CLARKSON POTTER/PUBLISHERS

NEW YORK

PEGGY PORSCHEN

photographs by Georgia Glynn Smith

simply spectacular cakes

beautiful designs for irresistible cakes and cookies

To my wonderful husband Bryn
and to my family, with all my love

Text and designs copyright © 2009 by Peggy Porschen
Photographs copyright © 2009 by Georgia Glynn Smith
Edited text copyright © 2009 by Quadrille Publishing Ltd

All rights reserved.
Published in the United States by Clarkson
Potter/Publishers, an imprint of the Crown Publishing
Group, a division of Random House, Inc., New York.
www.crownpublishing.com
www.clarksonpotter.com

CLARKSON POTTER is a trademark and POTTER with
colophon is a registered trademark of Random House, Inc.

Originally published in Great Britain as CAKE CHIC by
Quadrille Publishing Limited, London, in 2009.

Library of Congress Cataloging-in-Publication Data is
available upon request.

ISBN 978-0-307-46455-2

Printed in China

10 9 8 7 6 5 4 3 2 1

First American Edition

Contents

Cookies

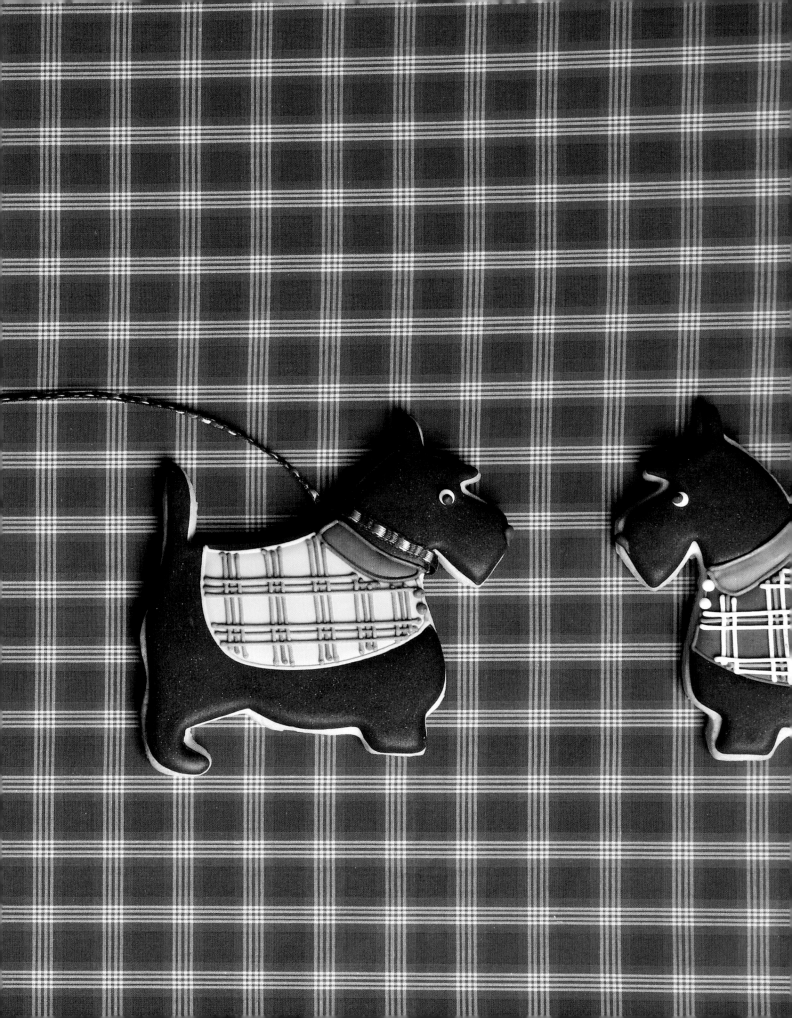

MAKES 12 PAIRS

Ballerina
pumps

When Chanel commissioned me to design party favors to celebrate the 50th anniversary of the ballerina pump I was delighted—cookies couldn't get more couture! They were served at a celebrity-studded tea party with each cookie bearing a guest's name iced along the middle.

INGREDIENTS

12 pairs ballet pump cookies made from ½ recipe quantity Vanilla Cookie Dough (page 110)
about heaped 1 cup Royal Icing (page 132)
    ivory, pink, dark brown, and black food colors

TOOLS

ballet pump templates (page 144)
paper pastry bags (page 134)
small bowls
small spatula
plastic wrap or resealable plastic bag
pair of scissors
12 sheets of wrapping paper (optional)
6 gift boxes (optional)
About 6 yards ribbon, ¾ inch wide (optional)

1 Start by mixing your icing colors, you will need:
2 pastry bags filled with nude royal icing (mix ivory, pink, and dark brown)—one soft-peak and one runny (page 132).
2 pastry bags filled with black icing—one soft-peak and one runny
1 pastry bag filled with runny cream-colored icing (use ivory)
2 pastry bags filled with ivory icing— one soft-peak and one runny.

2 Begin by piping the nude-colored outlines using soft-peak icing. Snip a small tip off the bag and pipe the inner and outer shapes of the pump in a steady and smooth line (see 1). Repeat for all the pumps and let dry.

3 Using the runny nude-colored icing, flood the space between the two outlines on each cookie (see 2) and let the icing dry.

4 Outline the shoe tips using soft-peak black icing (see 3).

5 Flood the central part of the cookies with the runny cream-colored icing and let dry (see 3).

6 Flood the middles of the tips with runny black icing (see 4); let dry.

7 Once all the colors on the cookies are dry, pipe the black bow detail using soft-peak icing (see 5).

8 For the tag, pipe a rectangle across the cream-colored middle using soft-peak ivory icing and flood it with runny ivory icing; let dry.

9 You can pipe a guest's name across the tag using black soft-peak icing. If you like, wrap each pair in pretty paper, put in gift boxes, and tie with ribbon.

little Black Dress

Every girl has one—what does yours look like? Mine was inspired by a 1950s' vintage Dior design. The secret of this cookie is to keep the actual dress design quite simple and then to add a pretty finishing touch by tying a chic little satin bow around the waist to match your party's color scheme. They make the perfect treat for any fashionista tea party!

INGREDIENTS

12 dress cookies (about 3¼ x 5 inches) made from 1 recipe quantity of Sugar Cookie Dough (page 110)

about heaped 1 cup Royal Icing (page 132)

black food color

small amount of water

TOOLS

dress cookie cutter (about 3¼ x 5 inches)

small bowl

small spatula

paper pastry bags (page 134)

plastic wrap or resealable plastic bag, to cover the icing

24 inches brightly colored satin ribbon, ⅛ inch wide

1 Put the royal icing in a small bowl and mix it with black food color to a deep black. Add a small amount of water until the icing is soft-peak consistency (page 132). Put some into a pastry bag. Keep the remaining icing covered.

2 Snip a small tip off the bag and pipe the outlines of the dresses in a steady, smooth line (see piping techniques on page 135). Keep the pastry bag covered in a plastic bag or in plastic wrap until later to prevent it from drying out.

3 Dilute the remaining icing with a few drops of water to a runny consistency (page 132). Put it in a fresh pastry bag.

4 Again, snip the tip off the bag and flood the cookie middles with the runny icing, being careful not to overflow the sides; let dry.

5 Once dry, pipe the details on your dresses using the remaining soft-peak royal icing.

6 Once completely dry, tie the ribbons around the waists with a little bow at the front of each.

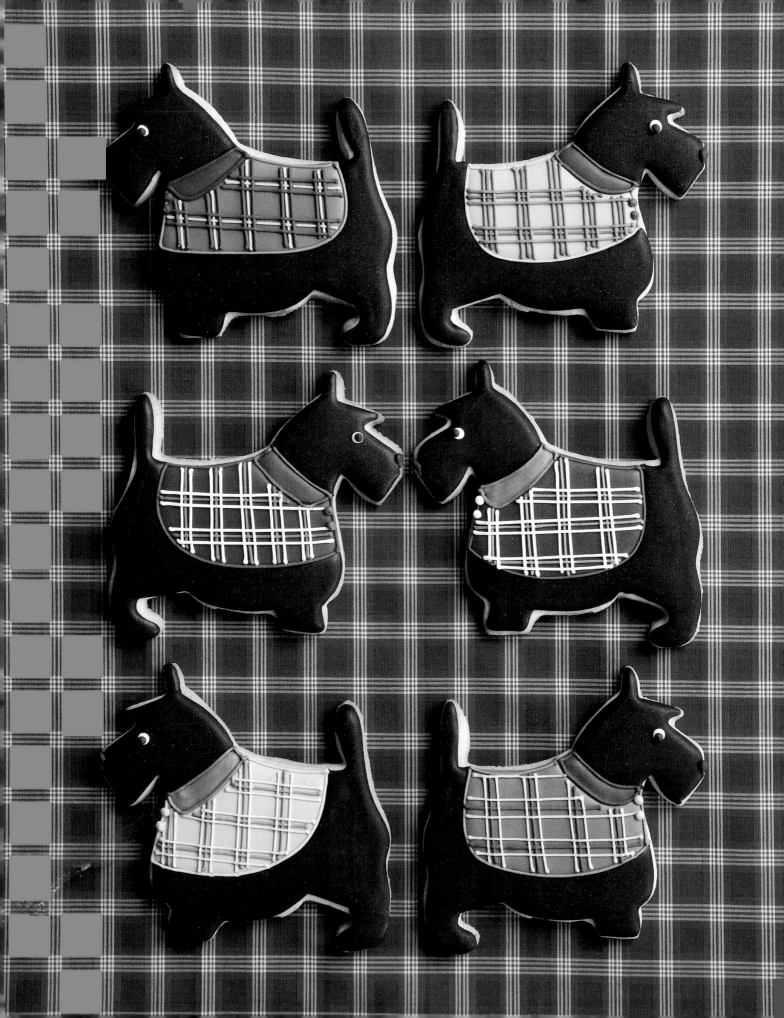

**MAKES 12
COOKIES**

best in *Show*

These Scotties make great gifts for dog lovers! You can bake them in the shape of your favorite breed, from Afghans to Salukis. There are plenty of different dog cookie cutters (see the suppliers list on page 137).

INGREDIENTS
12 dog cookies made from 1 quantity
of Vanilla Cookie Dough (page 110)
about 1¾ cups Royal Icing (page 132)
black, brown, ivory, purple, dark-
pink, and green food colors
small amount of water

TOOLS
dog cookie cutter (about 4¼ x 3¼
inches)
small bowls
small spatula
paper pastry bags (page 134)
plastic wrap or resealable plastic bag

1 Color a scant 1 cup royal icing black. Add a little water until soft-peak consistency is reached (page 132). Put a small amount in a pastry bag and cover the rest.

2 Snip a small tip off the bag and pipe the outlines, leaving space for jacket and collar. Pipe all black outlines first (see 1). If icing is left in the bag, keep in the resealable bag.

3 Make the remaining black icing runny (page 132) by adding a little water. Put in a fresh bag.

4 Snip a tip off the bag and fill the middles of the dogs with the runny icing (see 2), being careful not to overflow the sides; let dry.

5 Prepare your icing for the jackets. You will need:
1 bag with a little brown soft-peak;
1 bag with a little ivory soft-peak;
1 bag with a little purple soft-peak;
about 2 bags with purple runny;
1 bag with a little dark-pink soft-peak;

about 2 bags with dark-pink runny;
1 bag with a little green soft-peak;
About 2 bags with green runny.

6 Pipe the outlines for the jacket collars and jackets using soft-peak icing as shown (see 2); let dry.

7 Flood the jacket centers with the appropriate runny color (see 3) Let dry.

8 Flood the collars with the runny color (see 4); let dry.

9 Using soft-peak icing, pipe the outlines for the jacket and the collar (see 5), followed by the tartan designs. Mix and match colors as shown or to your taste (see 6). Let one color dry first before you pipe a different one on top, as they can bleed into one another if still wet.

MAKES 12
COOKIES

pretty Bows

These cookies suit girly get-togethers or bridal and baby showers. You can keep them plain with just a touch of luster, decorate them with dots, or embellish them with sugar pearls for a more sophisticated affair. They also look very chic in black and white—great for a cocktail party.

INGREDIENTS
12 small bow-shaped cookies (about 2½ inches) made from ½ recipe quantity of Vanilla Cookie Dough (page 110)
10 ounces Royal Icing (page 132)
ivory, pink, blue, and yellow food colors
small amount of water
ivory sugar pearls
Pearl Lustre Spray (PME)

TOOLS
bow cookie cutter (about 2½ inches)
small bowl
small spatula
small kitchen knife
paper pastry bags (page 134)
plastic wrap or resealable plastic bag, to cover the icing

FOR THE THIN PEARL-STUDDED BOWS
1 To make about 4 of these, heat the oven to 350°F.

2 Roll a small amount of dough to about ¼ inch thick. Cut out 4 strips ¼ inch wide and 5½ inches long.

3 Fold to make a bow as below and pinch in the middle.

4 Bake for 6 to 8 minutes with the 8 cut-out bow cookies; leave to cool on a wire rack.

5 Fill a pastry bag with a little soft-peak (page 132) white royal icing and pipe a thin line all along each of the pearl-studded bow cookies.

6 While the icing is still wet, stick a row of white sugar pearls on top of the icing; let dry.

FOR THE CUT-OUT BOWS
7 Prepare your icing colors and pastry bags. You will need:

2 bags with pale pink icing—1 with soft-peak and 1 with runny (page 132);
2 bags with pale blue icing—1 with soft-peak and 1 with runny;
2 bags with pale yellow icing—1 with soft-peak and 1 with runny;
1 bag with soft-peak ivory icing.

8 Start by piping the outlines: snip a small tip off the bag and pipe around the bow outlines in a steady, smooth line; let dry. If you have any icing left in your bags, keep them in resealable bags.

9 Flood the bow middles with runny icing in appropriate colors and let dry.

10 Pipe the outlines using the soft-peak icing in corresponding colors and place a cluster of sugar pearls in the middle. Alternatively, use soft-peak ivory icing to pipe very small dots on the outlines instead.

11 Finish by spraying a light dusting of pearl spray over the dry cookies.

Christmas
baubles

These beautiful baubles make ornaments for your Christmas tree that are both festive and sophisticated. They look amazing in any color combination, so for something more traditional use red, green, and white; or, for a bold statement, try fuchsia, burnt orange, and deep purple. Gingerbread has a very long shelf-life, so these decorative cookies also make wonderful gifts and stocking fillers.

INGREDIENTS

6 small (about 2½ inches) and 6 large (about 4½ inches) tree ornament cookies with holes at the top made from ½ recipe quantity of Gingerbread Dough (page 112)

about 1¾ cups Royal Icing (page 132)

pink, purple, and ivory food colors

small amount of water

silver sugar balls

TOOLS

small bowls

small spatula

paper pastry bags (page 134)

plastic wrap or resealable plastic bags to cover the icing

about 6½ yards purple satin ribbon, ¼ inch wide

1 Prepare you icing colors: for 2 small and 2 large baubles of each color (pink, purple, and ivory) you will need 1 small pastry bag filled with soft-peak icing and 1 slightly larger pastry bag filled with runny icing (page 132.)

2 First pipe all the outlines of the baubles using the soft-peak icing.

3 Then flood the bauble middles using the runny icing in the corresponding colors; let dry.

4 Once dry, pipe the details on top and embellish the designs with silver sugar pearls where shown while that icing is still wet. Let the icing dry completely.

5 Once dry, cut the ribbon into 12 pieces, thread them through the holes in the baubles, and tie them into a bow. Handle the cookies with care as they are very fragile.

MAKES 12
COOKIES

Silhouette cookies

These timelessly stylish silhouette cookies make great party favors for birthdays, engagements, and, in particular, weddings. Using profile photographs of the bride and groom—or guests—is a great way to personalize these wonderful gifts. Imagine the fun and laughter as your guests try to find their own silhouette! I chose chocolate on pastels for a retro-feel, but they also look very chic in black and white.

INGREDIENTS

12 oval (about 4 inches) cookies made from ½ recipe quantity Gingerbread Dough (page 112)

about 1¼ cups Royal Icing (page 132)

dark brown, blue, pink, and ivory food colors

small amount of water

small amount of vegetable shortening

edible gold luster dust

TOOLS

small bowls

small spatula

paper pastry bags (page 134)

sheet of cellophane or plastic sleeve

waxed paper

pencil

2-inch diameter face silhouette prints

soft artist's brush for dusting

plastic wrap or resealable plastic bags, to cover the icing

1 For the silhouettes you need 1 small pastry bag of brown soft-peak icing and 1 slightly larger bag filled with brown runny (page 132).

2 To make your own silhouette templates, place the photographs on a flat surface or a tray and place a piece of waxed paper over them. Trace the outlines with a pencil, then place a sheet of cellophane on top and rub in very thinly with the vegetable fat.

3 Using the soft-peak brown icing, first the trace all the outlines of the silhouette templates, then flood the middles with the runny brown icing. Let them dry overnight.

4 Next day, to ice the cookies, divide the remaining icing equally into 3 bowls and mix one each with pink, blue, and ivory (use a lot of the ivory to make it very creamy) food colors respectively. Add a little water, if

required, to get a soft-peak consistency. Fill a small amount of each color into a pastry bag and keep the remaining icing covered to prevent it from drying out.

5 Use these bags to outline 4 cookies in each color and squeeze the leftover icing back into their bowls. Add more water to make the icing runny, fill each color into a new bag, and flood the cookie middles.

6 Where required, let small dots of an opposite color drop into the icing while it is still wet, to create a spotty background pattern. Let the cookies dry completely.

7 For the golden cookies, brush the creamy golden iced cookies generously with the gold luster dust, using a soft artist brush.

8 Once the silhouettes are dry, stick them on top of the cookies with dabs of royal icing.

MAKES 30
COOKIES

i want
Candy

These retro cookies, inspired by traditional candies, add a fun factor to any party. For younger guests, mix primary colors; for grown-up parties, keep them classy by using, say, black, white and bright pink. They make great give-away treats for guests. Pile them into an old-fashioned sweet jar, mixed with sweets, or wrap in cellophane and decorate with ribbon.

INGREDIENTS

15 round cookies (about 1¼ inches in diameter) and 15 round (or oval) cookies (about 2 inches in diameter), made from 1 quantity of Sugar Cookie Dough (page 110)

black and pink food colors

about 1¾ cups Royal Icing (page 132)

small amount of water

about 1½ tablespoons each white, black, and pink sugar balls

EQUIPMENT

selection of small bowls

small spatula

paper pastry bags (page 134)

plastic wrap or a damp cloth to cover the icing

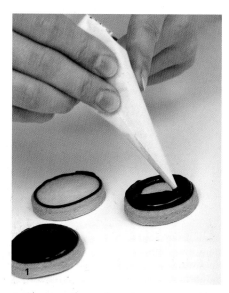

1 Choose the colors for your cookies and divide the icing equally into bowls, one per color. Using a clean spatula each time, mix each one with a small amount of food color to the desired tone and add a little water until the icing has soft-peak consistency (page 132). Fill a pastry bag of each.

2 Snip a small tip off the bag containing your chosen color for outlines and pipe the outline of each cookie in a steady, smooth line. When not in use, cover the bags with plastic wrap or a plastic bag to prevent them from drying out.

3 Once the icing outlines are dry, flood the middles: dilute a small amount of the corresponding icing color with some water to runny consistency (page 132) and use to fill a pastry bag. Snip a small tip of the bag and pipe the liquid icing into the middles, being careful not to overflow the sides (see 1).

4 If flooding sections in different colors, let one color dry first before flooding the next, to avoid them flowing together.

5 While the flooded icing is still wet, pipe the white dots on black-iced cookies to be dotted, so they sink into the background (see 2), and sprinkle cookies being decorated with sugar balls with the appropriately colored balls (see 3).

6 Once the other cookies are dry, pipe outlines and stripes, and so on, in the appropriate colors, using soft-peak icing.

Mini Cakes

Damask delights

Damask patterns have made a huge comeback, and I love the eclectic mix of different pattern and color possibilities. My little damask cakes make super-stylish treats for any cocktail party, presented on a colorful tray. These colors work particularly well for guests of both sexes, but they would also look beautiful in softer shades or tone-on-tone combinations.

INGREDIENTS

16 Fondant Fancies made from an 8-inch square Victoria Sponge Cake flavored to your choice, dipped in eggplant-colored fondant icing (pages 114 and 129-30) made using purple and burgundy food colors
about ¾ cup Royal Icing (page 132)
burgundy, baby blue, and lemon yellow food colors
small amount of water

TOOLS

about 16 silver metallic muffin cases
2 small bowls
small spatula
paper pastry bags (page 134)
plastic wrap

1 Place the fondant fancies in the silver paper cases as described on page 130.

2 Place half the royal icing in a small bowl and, using a spatula, mix it with the burgundy food color, then add a few drops of water until the icing reaches soft-peak consistency (page 132).

3 Fill some of the icing into a pastry bag and keep the rest in the bowl, covered with plastic wrap to prevent it from drying out so you can use it later, if required.

4 Snip a small tip off the pastry bag and pipe the pink design on half the fondant fancies.

5 Repeat steps 2 and 3 using baby blue and lemon yellow to mix a bright lime green color and pipe that on the other half of the fancies.

6 Store at room temperature 3 to 5 days in a cake box or wrapped in foil.

**MAKES 10
MINI CAKES**

Cameo
cakes

If there were a modern Marie-Antoinette, these would most definitely be her favorite cakes. I used antique cameo brooches as inspiration for these ultrachic cakes. Perfect for tea parties in Versailles, don't you think? You can also make your own molds from a vintage piece of jewelry, using a specialty food-safe molding gel.

INGREDIENTS

12 oval miniature cakes, made from a 12-inch square Victoria Sponge Cake (page 114), flavored to your choice, covered with 3¼ pounds marzipan and a thin layer of shell-pink rolled fondant (about 2¼ pounds)
about 18 ounces ready-to-use white rolled fondant
small amount of gum tragacanth
small amount of vegetable shortening
black food color
confectioners' sugar or cornstarch, for dusting
edible glue
small amount of Royal Icing (page 132)

TOOLS

plastic wrap
2 or 3 rubber cameo molds (available at decorating supply stores)
small rolling pin
small kitchen knife
small nonstick plastic board
oval cutter, about 1½ x 2 inches
Stayfresh multi-mat
small artist's brush
paper pastry bags (page 134)
about 3½ yards black satin ribbon, ⅜ inches wide

1 Knead the white rolled fondant with a small amount of gum tragacanth until stretchy, smooth, and pliable. Wrap it in plastic wrap until needed, to prevent it from drying out.

2 Lightly grease each of the cameo molds with a small quantity of shortening.

3 Roll a hazelnut-size piece of the rolled fondant for each mold into a ball, place it over the middle of the prepared mold, and push it thoroughly into the mold. Level out the top with a small rolling pin, then trim off the excess fondant with a small kitchen knife.

4 To release the fondant from the mold, bend each mold inside out and the fondant should drop out; let dry.

5 Mix the remaining white rolled fondant with black food color.

6 On a plastic board lightly dusted with confectioners' sugar or cornstarch, roll out the black fondant to a thickness of about ⅛ inch.

7 Using the oval cutter, cut out 10 ovals of black rolled fondant (one for each cake). Brush an area on top of each cake about the same size as the oval with edible glue and place one of the black rolled-fondant ovals on top of each cake. Keep the ovals not being worked on under the multi-mat to prevent them from drying out.

8 Using edible glue in the same way, now stick the cameos on top of the rolled-fondant ovals.

9 To make the bows, cut a few thin strips of rolled fondant with a knife and shape into loops, securing the knot with a tiny brushing of edible glue; let dry about 30 minutes.

10 Meanwhile, mix the royal icing with a little bit of water to a soft-peak consistency (page 132) and fill a pastry bag with it.

11 Cut the black ribbon into pieces that fit around the bottom of each cake and secure in place at the back with a dab of royal icing.

12 Snip a small piece off the tip of the pastry bag and pipe the different swag and pearl borders around the bottom—half on, half off the ribbon. This gives you a great visual effect.

13 Next, while the icing is still wet, pipe a pearl border around the black edge of each cameo and then place a bow either at the top or the bottom of the cameo.

14 You can finish some of the bows by piping dropping pearls down from the knot, if you like.

**MAKES 18
MINI CAKES**

mini *Orangery* cakes

These cakes are inspired by the ornate architecture of some beautiful orangeries I have been lucky enough to visit. A bit of time and patience will be needed to master the dome-making technique, but they are well worth the effort. These caged blooms work well at coming-of-age or engagement parties.

INGREDIENTS

18 round miniature (2 inches) cakes, made from 12 inch square Victoria Sponge Cake (page 114), flavored to your choice, covered with slightly less than 2 pounds marzipan and a thin layer of white rolled fondant (about 2¼ pounds)

small amount of vegetable shortening

scant ¾ cup Royal Icing (page 132)

about 7 ounces ready-to-use white rolled fondant

about 7 ounces White Gum Paste (SK)

burgundy, moss green, and violet food colors

TOOLS

a few dome-shaped stainless steel pastry molds, 2½ inch diameter

baking tray

several small plastic bowls

small spatula

paper pastry bags (see page 134)

pair of scissors

foam mat

plastic wrap

clear plastic pocket (from office supply stores)

small nonstick plastic board with holes for "Mexican hat" backs (Celboard)

small rolling pin

small stephanotis blossom cutter

Dresden tool

about 5½ yards Malibu blue satin ribbon, ⅜ inch wide

Stayfresh multi-mat

small rose leaf cutter

flower foam pad

rose leaf veining mat

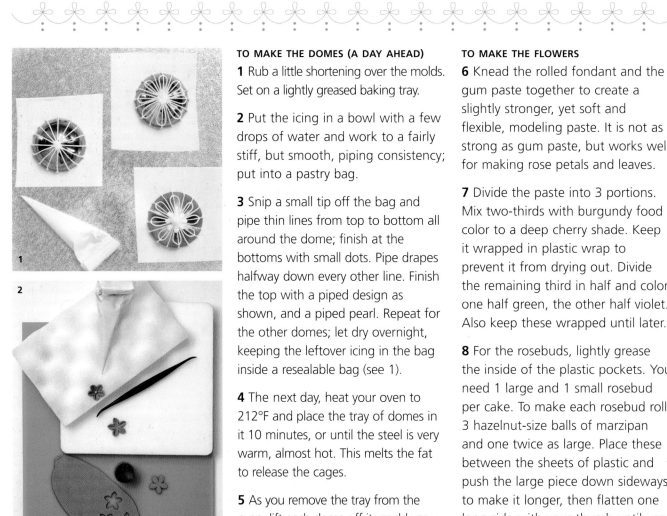

TO MAKE THE DOMES (A DAY AHEAD)

1 Rub a little shortening over the molds. Set on a lightly greased baking tray.

2 Put the icing in a bowl with a few drops of water and work to a fairly stiff, but smooth, piping consistency; put into a pastry bag.

3 Snip a small tip off the bag and pipe thin lines from top to bottom all around the dome; finish at the bottoms with small dots. Pipe drapes halfway down every other line. Finish the top with a piped design as shown, and a piped pearl. Repeat for the other domes; let dry overnight, keeping the leftover icing in the bag inside a resealable bag (see 1).

4 The next day, heat your oven to 212°F and place the tray of domes in it 10 minutes, or until the steel is very warm, almost hot. This melts the fat to release the cages.

5 As you remove the tray from the oven, lift each dome off its mold very carefully and place it on the foam mat.

TO MAKE THE FLOWERS

6 Knead the rolled fondant and the gum paste together to create a slightly stronger, yet soft and flexible, modeling paste. It is not as strong as gum paste, but works well for making rose petals and leaves.

7 Divide the paste into 3 portions. Mix two-thirds with burgundy food color to a deep cherry shade. Keep it wrapped in plastic wrap to prevent it from drying out. Divide the remaining third in half and color one half green, the other half violet. Also keep these wrapped until later.

8 For the rosebuds, lightly grease the inside of the plastic pockets. You need 1 large and 1 small rosebud per cake. To make each rosebud roll 3 hazelnut-size balls of marzipan and one twice as large. Place these between the sheets of plastic and push the large piece down sideways to make it longer, then flatten one long side with your thumb until very thin (see 3). For the other petals,

begin to push one of the smaller pieces down with your thumb, starting from the middle to one side, until it forms a round petal, with one thick and one thin edge; repeat with the other balls. Taking the large petal first, roll it into a spiral shape, thin edge up (see 4). Take one of the smaller petals, thin edge up, and lay it around the the middle over the seam. Then tuck the second petal slightly inside the first and the third inside the second petal, and squeeze it around the middle (see 5). Slightly curve the edges of the petals out with your fingertips. Make sure they are small enough to fit under the cages. Keep the petals not being shaped under the multi-mat until they are all shaped.

9 To make the leaves, roll out the green paste to about 1/16 inch thick and stamp out 2 leaves per cake (36 in total), using the small rose leaf cutter. Place them on a flower foam pad and gently stretch and thin the edges with the Dresden tool. Press each leaf in the rose leaf veiner and shape slightly with your fingers for a natural look. Keep the leaves you haven't worked on under the multi-mat until all are shaped.

10 For the little violet-colored blossoms, roll a small piece of violet paste out on the plastic board until about 1/16 inch thick (see 2). You will need to cut out 3 blossoms per cake (54 in total)

11 Working with one blossom at a time, while it is still soft, place it on

the foam pad and run the Dresden tool along each petal to emboss it; let them dry. Keep the blossoms you haven't worked on under the multi-mat until they are all shaped.

12 Once the blossoms dry, pipe a small dot of the reserved white (or color it appropriately) icing onto the middles.

TO ASSEMBLE AND FINISH
13 Cut the ribbon into pieces to fit around the bottom of each cake

and secure with a little royal icing at the back.

14 Arrange a cluster of rosebuds, leaves, and blossoms on the top of each cake, leaving an edge on which the domes can rest.

15 Finally, pipe a few dots of icing around the edge and carefully place the dome on top. You can use trimmings to make extra rosebuds, leaves, and blossoms for decoration.

mini Monogram cakes

This is a great and relatively easy idea for making personalised cakes for any occasion. For example, you can use a single monogram, a number to celebrate someone's birthday, or the interlinked initials of a couple for a wedding anniversary. You can also use different letters to spell out a message or even use the cakes as table place cards for your guests using their initials. With a generous 3-inch size, these cakes can also be served as desserts. The templates on pages 142-3 will provide you with a simple but chic alphabet and border designs so you can make up your own variations.

INGREDIENTS

8 round marbled miniature cakes, with a diameter of 3 inches made from a 10 inch square Marbled Sponge Cake (page 118), layered with vanilla buttercream, then covered with marzipan and pale brown rolled fondant (page 126).

scant 1 cup Royal Icing (page 132)

dark brown food color

small amount of water

TOOLS

alphabet and border templates (page 142-3)

waxed paper

pencil

scriber tool

small bowl

small spatula

paper pastry bags (page 134)

plastic wrap

about 3 yards dark brown grosgrain ribbon, 1 inch wide

1

2

3

1 Choose your monogram letter(s) or numeral(s) from the template and trace onto a small piece of waxed paper with a pencil.

2 Center the paper on top of each cake and carefully trace the image through the paper onto the icing of the cake using the scriber tool (see 1).

3 Choose a border design from page 142 and also trace this on to

the paper as before. Place it neatly around the edge of the cake and trace it on to the cake as well.

4 Prepare pastry bags filled with soft-peak and one with runny dark brown icing (page 132).

5 Snip a fine tip off the bag of soft-peak icing and pipe along the outside of the letters (see 2) and trace the border (see 3).

6 Then use the runny icing to flood the middles of the monograms.

7 Place the ribbon around the bottoms and attach with small dabs of icing.

8 Store 3 to 5 days at room temperature in a cake box or wrapped in foil.

Cherry Blossom bites

Cherry blossoms are one of my favorite flowers as they are so delicate, fresh, and pretty. These fondant fancies suit a tea party marking the arrival of spring. Not only do they look divine, but they also taste heavenly—the fruity-fresh Morello cherry jam and the bittersweet chocolate perfectly complement one another, and the smooth fondant icing helps create a wonderful melt-in-your-mouth texture.

INGREDIENTS

16 Fondant Fancies made from an
8-inch square Victoria Sponge Cake
    flavored with vanilla, filled with one
    layer of Morello cherry jam, then
    dipped in pastel pink fondant icing
    (pages 114 and 129).
about 2 ounces white gum paste
burgundy food color
small amount of vegetable shortening
small amount of cornstarch for dusting
7 ounces couverture chocolate,
    chopped
pink edible dust color
1 tablespoon Royal Icing (page 132)
small amount of water

TOOLS

small microwaveable bowl
small spatula
small nonstick plastic board
small rolling pin
foam flower pad
five-petal flower cutters in 3 sizes,
    ranging from about ¾ to 1½ inches
    in diameter
Stayfresh multi-mat
dogbone tool
plastic spatula
fine artist's brush
paper pastry bags (page 134)
pair of scissors
plastic wrap or resealable plastic bag
microwaveable bowl
microwave
digital thermometer
damp kitchen cloth
wire rack
waxed paper
plastic paint palette

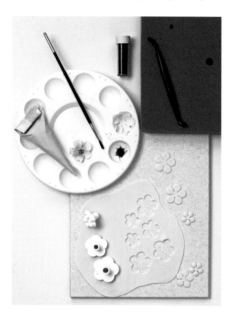

MAKE ABOUT 30 CHERRY BLOSSOMS (ABOUT 10 IN EACH SIZE) AT LEAST ONE DAY IN ADVANCE

1 Mix the gum paste with a tiny drop of burgundy food color to a very pale pink. If the paste is very stiff and sticky, add a dab of the shortening and knead it until it is smooth and pliable.

2 Lightly grease the nonstick plastic board with a small amount of the shortening and roll out the pale pink paste until it is about 1/16 inch thick. Cut out the flower shapes using the five-petal flower cutters and remove the trimmings. (Keep these wrapped in plastic wrap or in a resealable plastic bag to prevent the paste from drying out.)

3 Place one flower shape at a time on the foam flower pad and keep the remaining flower shapes on the plastic board covered with the Stayfresh multi-mat to prevent them from drying out.

4 To shape the petals, move the thicker end of the dogbone tool gently across each one until it is thin and slightly frilly, being very careful not to tear it.

5 As all the petals are shaped, place the flower into the well of the plastic palette that has been lightly dusted with cornstarch to prevent the flower sticking to it.

6 Repeat steps 3 to 5 for all the remaining flowers and let them dry at least 4 hours, or overnight.

7 Once dry, lightly dust the flower centers with the dark pink dust color using the fine artist's brush. To make the color dust slightly paler, mix it with a small amount of cornstarch.

8 Mix about half the royal icing with the burgundy food color and a small amount of water to a soft-peak consistency (page 132). Put it in a paper pastry bag, snip a small tip off the bag, and pipe small dots in the middle of each flower.

TO TEMPER THE CHOCOLATE

9 Place 5 ounces of the chocolate in a microwaveable bowl and melt it gently in a microwave at medium heat. Be careful not to overheat it, because chocolate burns easily. Check the temperature with a thermometer; it should be melted and between 111° and 118°F.

10 Once it has reached the required temperature, stir the remaining chocolate into the melted chocolate to cool it down to 82°F while stirring.

11 Once the chocolate has cooled down, gently warm it again to 90° to 93°F, and the chocolate should now be tempered. (You can test it by dipping the blade of a spatula into the chocolate—it should set within a few minutes and have a silky, satiny texture.)

TO DIP THE FONDANT FANCIES IN THE CHOCOLATE

12 Once the chocolate has been tempered, have a damp kitchen cloth at hand, lightly wet your fingers with it and pick up one fondant fancy at a time. (This stops your fingers from sticking to the fondant.) Dip the bottom of the fancy into the chocolate until covered.

13 Place each fancy on a wire rack a few minutes to let excess chocolate drip off. Transfer the fancies to a sheet of waxed paper and leave until the chocolate sets.

14 Repeat for all the remaining fondant fancies.

TO FINISH

15 Put the remaining white icing into a paper pastry bag and use it to stick the cherry blossoms randomly on top of the fondant fancies.

16 Store at room temperature 3 to 5 days in an airtight container.

**MAKES 4
MINI CAKES**

peggy's *Purses*

There is something about designer handbags we girls simply can't resist. Although novelty cakes are not usually my thing, I couldn't help but wonder how my own signature purses would look if made from cake. They make wonderful birthday treats for girlfriends and are surprisingly simple to make. Replace my monogram with a friend's initial to make it her own.

INGREDIENTS

one 8-inch square Victoria Sponge Cake (this will hold the shape best), flavored to your choice (page 114)

about 1⅔ pounds marzipan

about 1 cup buttercream, flavored to your choice (page 120)

about 1⅔ pounds ready-to-use white rolled fondant

dark brown, dusky pink, and ivory food paste colors

small amount of gum tragacanth

small amount of vegetable shortening

small amount of clear alcohol or edible glue

edible pearl luster dust or pearl luster spray

about 1 tablespoon Royal Icing (page 132)

small amount of water

TOOLS

cake leveler

4-inch round pastry cutter

small kitchen knife

small rolling pin

small spatula

pair of cake smoothers

small bowls

spatula

plastic wrap

resealable plastic bag

design wheeler (from PME)

pastry brush

2 small round cutters (about ¾ inch and 1¼ inches in diameter)

soft artist's brush (if using pearl luster dust)

paper pastry bags (page 134)

1 Trim the top and bottom crust off the sponge cake, using the cake leveler. Your trimmed sponge should have a depth of about 1¾ inches Divide the cake into 4 even squares.

2 For the round bags, cut 3 semi-circles from 3 pieces of cake (see 1). For the square handbag, cut the remaining sponge to a slightly oblong shape of about 3 x 3¼ inches.

3 Stand the cakes upright and cut the wide sides at a slight angle to narrow them at the top (see 2 and 3).

4 For each cake, roll out a piece of marzipan about 4½ inches deep, 8 inches wide, and ⅛ to 1/16 inch thick. Place a piece of cake on one of these pieces and trim the marzipan to its width (see 4); reserve trimmings.

5 Now lay the sponge on its side on top of the marzipan and cut it along the cake edge. Repeat for the other side; it should fit exactly.

6 To cover the top edge, cut some marzipan trimmings to fit (see 5).

7 Spread buttercream thinly along the top of the bag and place the

marzipan on top. Trim the ends with a knife as they may have stretched.

8 Cover the bottom and sides of the cake thinly with buttercream, center it on top of the large cut piece of marzipan, and wrap that around the sides (see 6).

9 Gently shape the cake sides using the cake smoothers (see 7). Repeat for the remaining purse cakes and let the marzipan firm overnight.

10 Mix 10 ounces rolled fondant with dark brown food color to a chocolate color, 10 ounces with dusky pink to a light pink, and the remaining fondant with a little ivory. To keep these fresh and soft, wrap in plastic wrap until ready to use.

11 Mix about 2 ounces each of the pale pink fondant and the chocolate-brown fondant with about ½ teaspoon of gum tragacanth and knead it with a small amount of shortening until smooth.

12 To cover the cakes with fondant, roll out pale pink, ivory, and chocolate-brown paste ⅛ to 1/16 inch and large enough to cover the cakes.

13 Brush each cake with alcohol and cover with the appropriate colored fondant by gently pushing down the sides with your hands (see 8); trim off excess and polish with smoothers.

14 While the fondant is still soft, for the brown and square pale pink purses run the stitching wheel of the design wheeler along the edges to emboss a stitched pattern.

TO DECORATE THE BROWN HANDBAG

15 Roll out more pale pink fondant and cut out a half-disc using the cutter used to cut out the sponge pieces, plus a small circle about 1¼ inches in diameter for the monogram.

16 Brush the area that will be covered with the "flap" with a thin layer of alcohol or glue and stick the pale pink half-disc of paste on top.

17 Repeat steps 15 and 16 (without making a smaller circle) to cover the pink flap with a slightly smaller flap made from the brown fondant. After that, stick the smaller pink circle on top of the brown flap.

18 To make the pale pink handles, roll the pale pink fondant mixed with the

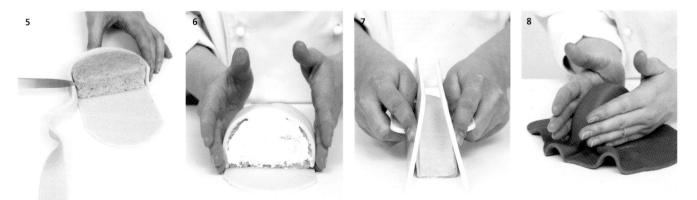

gum tragacanth until about ⅛ inch thick and large enough to cut out 2 even strips, each about 2½ x ½ inches.

19 Trim the ends of both strips to a V-shape and curve them with your fingers; let set a couple of hours.

TO DECORATE THE IVORY HANDBAG

20 Roll out a long thin piece of the chocolate-brown fondant mixed with the gum tragacanth and cut it into a thin strip about 1¼ inches wide and long enough to fit around the base of the purse. Brush the bottom with a thin layer of alcohol or glue and stick the strip around it.

21 Cut out another two 1¾-inch-long pieces for the handles; let dry in a curved shape a couple of hours.

22 For the fondant discs, roll a little pale pink fondant to ¹⁄₁₆ inch thick and cut out 1 to 15 discs using the 1¾-inch cutter; brush with pearl luster.

23 Carefully brush the back of the dots with alcohol or glue and stick them across the sides of the ivory purse, trimming those that overlap with a knife to join the edges.

TO DECORATE THE PALE PINK HALF-ROUND HANDBAG

24 Repeat steps 20 and 21, allowing extra fondant to make more strips for the sides and the flap.

25 To make the bow, cut out 2 more strips that are slightly wider— ¾ inch wide and 2½ inches long.

26 Pinch one of the strips in the middle and at the ends, fold ends toward the middle, and stick with a little glue. Cut a short piece off the second strip and wrap it around the middle of the bow, use a little glue to help it stick, if necessary. Pinch the leftover strip of paste in the middle and bend it halfway over to a V-shape and trim the tails at an angle. (Hat Boxes, page 90, step 11.)

TO DECORATE THE PALE PINK SQUARE PURSE

27 Make a chocolate-brown flap as in steps 15 and 16 (except do not make the small circle).

28 Cover the bottom of the purse with a very thin strip made from the pale pink fondant mixed with gum tragacanth, as in step 20.

29 To make the bow, repeat steps 25 and 26 using pale pink fondant mixed with gum tragacanth.

TO FINISH

30 Once all the handles are dry, divide the royal icing into 3 portions and color them pale pink, ivory, and chocolate-brown. Add a little water for a soft-peak consistency (page 132).

31 Secure the handles on the purses with a dab of matching royal icing.

32 Using the chocolate-brown icing, pipe a row of little dots around the pale pink discs on the ivory purse. Then pipe the initial onto the disc of the chocolate-brown purse, the tiny dots all over the sides of the pale pink square bag, and the little buttons on the handles on both pink bags.

33 Using the bag with the pale pink icing, pipe the swag border along the edge of the brown flap for the square pale pink bag, and the buttons on the handles of the ivory and the chocolate brown bags.

34 Stick the bows on to the pink bags with glue or icing.

**MAKES 12
CUPCAKES**

Cupcakes
in bloom

These stunning hydrangea cupcakes will not fail to delight! Admittedly, I might have gone a little bit over the top, but when I started arranging the individual blossoms on top of the cupcakes I just couldn't resist of adding more and more. I promise you will be showered with praise and hardly anyone will believe that the flowers are made of sugar, let alone that there is a cake underneath. Each cupcake is decorated with more than 15 hand-crafted blossoms, making this design undoubtedly a labor of love.

INGREDIENTS

12 cupcakes, baked in silver metallic muffin cases, made from ½ recipe Victoria Sponge Cake, flavored to your choice, soaked with syrup, and iced with fondant icing to match the colors of the flowers: 2 soft pink, 2 cerise pink, 2 lilac, 2 lavender, 2 burgundy and 2 purple (pages 114 and 131)
about 10 ounces white gum paste
small amount of vegetable shortening
burgundy and violet food colors
cornflour blue food color
burgundy, pink, and purple edible dust colors
about 3 tablespoons Royal Icing (page 132)
small amount of water

TOOLS

small bowls
plastic wrap or resealable plastic bags
small nonstick plastic board
small rolling pin
hydrangea flower cutter and petal veiner
piece of egg crate foam
Stayfresh multi-mat
fine artist's brush
paper pastry bags (page 134)
pair of scissors
small saucepan

MAKE THE HYDRANGEA BLOSSOMS AT LEAST ONE DAY IN ADVANCE

1 Knead the gum paste with a small dab of shortening until soft and pliable, then divide it into 6 equal portions.

2 Mix one portion with the burgundy food color to a soft pink, a second with a little more burgundy food color to a cherry pink, a third with violet food color to a lilac, a fourth with a little more violet to a purple, a fifth with a mixture of grape or violet and a tiny amount of cornflour blue to a lavender, and, finally, one with burgundy and violet to a deep burgundy color. Of course, you can create your own shades and color variations, but make sure the colors of the flowers match with the colors of the fondant icings. Always keep the paste you are not using covered in plastic wrap or in a resealable plastic bag to prevent it from drying out.

3 Lightly grease the nonstick plastic board with a small amount of shortening and roll one of the paste colors out to a thickness of 1/16 inch.

4 For 2 cupcakes of the same color, cut out about 30 hydrangea blossoms in total, using the hydrangea flower cutter.

5 Remove the excess paste from the plastic board and keep it covered in plastic wrap or in a resealable plastic bag to prevent it from drying out.

6 Take one blossom at a time and squeeze it between the 2 veining mats, then carefully remove it and place it inside a well of the profile foam sheet and let it dry. Repeat this process for the rest of the hydrangea blossoms and let them dry at least 4 hours, or ideally overnight. Keep the petals to be transferred to the profile foam sheet covered with the Stayfresh multi-mat to prevent them from drying out.

7 Once dry, dust the petal tips lightly with the dusting colors, using the fine artist's brush to create the natural shadings that are so characteristic of hydrangea. As all the colors work well together you can create your own variations. For example, use the pink dust on the lavender blossoms, the burgundy on the purple blossoms, and the purple dust on the pink blossoms. You can also mix the dust colors with each other to create even more different shades.

8 Once all the blossoms are dusted, prepare one pastry bag with soft-peak royal icing (page 132) to match each of the colors of the fondant icing and the flowers.

9 Snip a small tip off each bag and use the icing to stick the individual blossoms on top of the cupcakes, making sure you are using the same color of icing as that of the blossoms and the cupcake. Start by sticking the first blossom centered on the top and then arrange other blossoms all around, row by row. If you have any gaps, fill them by breaking off individual petals and sticking them into the gaps.

10 Put a small amount of water into a saucepan and bring it to a boil. As the steam is evaporating, hold each decorated cupcake over the steam for literally 2 seconds—this brings the colors of the petal dust to life and make the hydrangea blooms look even more realistic. Be careful not to steam them too long, because this can melt the icing and burn your hands!

11 Once all the flowers have been steamed, pipe small dots of icing in a matching color into all the blossom middles.

12 To store, keep these at room temperature 3to 5 days in a cake box.

**MAKES 12
CUPCAKES**

Dots and Bows

One of my most popular designs, these pretty and elegant cupcakes are very easy to make and work wonderfully for almost any type of celebration. For weddings, why not try a white-on-white color scheme, and for a little girl's name day pastel pink and white looks adorable.

INGREDIENTS

12 cupcakes made from ½ recipe quantity Victoria Sponge Cake, flavored to choice, baked in silver muffin cases, soaked with syrup, and iced with pale green fondant icing (pages 114 and 131)

about 4 ounces ready-to-use white rolled fondant

about 4 ounces gum paste

small amount of vegetable shortening

cornstarch for dusting

small amount of edible glue

pearl luster spray

small amount of Royal Icing (page 132)

small amount of water

TOOLS

small nonstick plastic board

small rolling pin

Stayfresh multi-mat

small kitchen knife

fine artist's brush

waxed paper

paper pastry bags (page 134)

small spatula

plastic wrap

1 Mix the fondant with the gum paste and a small dab of shortening, and knead it until smooth and pliable.

2 On a plastic board lightly dusted with cornstarch, roll out the paste until ⅛ inch thick and cut it into 12 strips, about ⅜ inch wide and 4 inches long.

3 Taking one strip at a time (keeping the rest covered), pinch it together in the middle and at both ends.

4 Brush the middle with a small amount of edible glue, fold both ends toward the middle and pinch them together. Repeat this process.

5 To cover the bow middles, roll out some more paste to the same thickness as before and cut it into 12 strips each ½ inch wide and 1¼ inches long.

6 Taking one strip at a time (and keeping the rest covered), brush it with a thin layer of glue. Wrap one strip around the middle of each bow.

7 For the bow tails, roll out more paste and cut out 12 more strips to the same size as in step 2.

8 Taking one strip at a time (and keeping the rest covered), pinch it in the middle, then fold the tails over so they form a V-shape and cut the ends off the strips at an angle.

9 Place all the bow pieces on a sheet of waxed paper and spray them with the Pearl Lustre Spray to give them a satin shimmer.

10 While the tails are still soft, using the edible glue, stick them on top of the cupcakes with the tails toward the front, then stick on the bows centered on top.

11 Mix the royal icing with a small amount of water to a soft-peak consistency (page 132) and put it in a pastry bag.

12 Snip a fine tip off the bag and pipe small dots all over the surface.

Ice Crystal cakes

Inspired by Victorian tree ornaments these beautifully ornate cakes are timelessly elegant and will add a touch of magic not only to your Christmas table but also to any winter-themed occasion. The symmetrical patterns are very easy to pipe in stages, simply by using the templates on page 141. If you prefer, you can also create your own patterns and just use my templates as a guide. To show how it's done I have picked one cake as an example below. The technique of repeating and building up symmetrically piped patterns on top of one another is the same for all designs.

INGREDIENTS

eight 3-inch round miniature cakes made from a 10-inch square cake of your choice, covered with marzipan and a mixture of ivory and pale blue rolled fondant (pages 114-18)

Pearl Lustre Spray (PME)

about 2 tablespoons Royal Icing (page 132)

small amount of water

silver sugar pearls

white sugar sprinkles

TOOLS

Ice Crystal Templates (page 141)

waxed paper

scriber tool

small snowflake cutter (about 1¼ inches diameter)

small spatula

paper pastry bags (page 134)

about 3 yards white grosgrain ribbon, ⅜ inch wide

4 Mix about 1 tablespoon of royal icing with a small amount of water to a soft-peak consistency (page 132) and put it in a pastry bag. Snip a small tip off the bag and begin by piping the outline of the snowflake and the straight lines and dots from the middle toward the edge of the cake (see 2).

5 Continue to pipe the scroll designs in between the lines and dots (see 3). Embellish with silver sugar pearls at this stage for the other designs where appropriate.

6 Mix the remaining royal icing with a little more water to give a runny consistency (page 132), put it in a pastry bag, and use to flood the middle of the snowflake.

7 While the icing is still wet, sprinkle the white sugar sprinkles on top and let the icing dry (see 4).

8 Once dry, shake the excess sprinkles off the cake and stick a piece of ribbon around the bottom of the cake, securing it with a blob of royal icing.

2 3 4

French fancies

My inspiration for these designs comes from an old French patisserie book I used to study during my training at Le Cordon Bleu. The piped chocolate designs have an appealing retro-feel and are easy to achieve with simple piping techniques. This type of fondant fancy is also known as a "petit four," from the French for oven, and is traditionally layered with lots of very thin slices of sponge and buttercream. I used a wonderfully fragrant orange sponge with orange buttercream for these.

INGREDIENTS

16 Fondant Fancies dipped variously in pastel pink, yellow, blue, green, and lilac fondant icing (page 129), made from an 8-inch square Victoria Sponge Cake flavored with orange zest and filled with 3 layers of orange buttercream (pages 114 and 120)

7 ounces couverture chocolate, chopped

1 tablespoon Royal Icing (page 132)

dark brown food color (I use paste color)

small amount of water

TOOLS

small microwaveable bowl

microwave

digital thermometer

small spatula

damp kitchen cloth

wire rack

waxed paper

paper pastry bag (page 134)

pair of scissors

TO TEMPER THE CHOCOLATE

1 Place 5 ounces of the chocolate in a microwaveable bowl and melt it gently in a microwave on medium heat. Be careful not to overheat it, because chocolate burns easily. Check the temperature with a thermometer; it should be melted at between 111° to 118°F.

2 Once it has reached the required temperature, stir the remaining chocolate into the melted chocolate. This will cool it down to 82°F.

3 Once the chocolate has cooled, gently warm it again to 90° to 93°F. The chocolate should now be tempered. (You can test it by dipping the blade of a spatula into it—it should set on the blade within a few minutes and have a silky, satiny texture.)

TO DIP THE FONDANT FANCIES IN THE CHOCOLATE

4 Once the chocolate has been tempered, have a damp kitchen cloth at hand, slightly wet your fingers with it, and pick up one fondant fancy at a time. (This stops your fingers from sticking to the fondant.) Dip the bottom of each fancy into the chocolate until well covered.

5 Place each fancy on a wire rack a few minutes to let excess chocolate drip off. Transfer the fancies to a sheet of waxed paper and leave until the chocolate sets.

TO FINISH

6 Mix the royal icing with the dark brown food color and a bit of water to a soft-peak consistency (page 132). Put it into a pastry bag.

7 Snip a small tip off the bag and pipe the different designs directly onto the fondant fancies.

8 Store at room temperature 3 to 5 days in an airtight container.

Large Cakes

pure *White* perfection

The inspiration for this cake, perhaps obviously, came from a wedding dress. The flowers are so simple to make and, yet, they are so effective. Their sheer abundance is complemented by piped swirls, which give a very sophisticated feel. This cake is perfect for a special birthday or anniversary party.

INGREDIENTS

6-inch round cake, flavored to your
    choice (pages 114-122), iced with
    1¼ pounds marzipan and 10 ounces
    ready-to-use white rolled fondant
about 9 ounces white gum paste
small amount of vegetable shortening
Pearl Lustre Spray (PME) or edible pearl
luster
    dust
scant 1 cup Royal Icing (page 132)

TOOLS

3 small circle cutters, ranging in
    diameter from ½ to ¾ inch
small rolling pin
small nonstick plastic board
Stayfresh multi-mat
bulbous cone or frilling tool
soft artist's brush (if using luster dust)
8-inch round cake board covered with
    1½ pounds white rolled fondant
    (page 131)
about 1¼ yards white satin ribbon
    ¾-inch wide
pair of scissors
small plastic bowl
small spatula
paper pastry bags (page 134)
tilting turntable

TO MAKE THE FLOWERS

1 The cake uses 3 different sizes of 5-petal flowers and you need about 10 in each size. To make the individual petals, use circular cutters in 3 different sizes, ranging from ½ to ¾ inch.

2 Roll a small amount of white gum paste out on a plastic board, lightly greased with the shortening, to a thickness of about ¹⁄₁₆ inch.

3 Cut out 5 or 6 petals in each size at a time (see 1). Keep the remaining paste covered with the Stayfresh multi-mat to prevent it from drying out.

4 Now roll each individual petal out again using the bulbous cone or frilling tool until it is so thin you can almost see through it, but still keeping its shape (see 2). Now that the petal is very thin, pinch it together at the bottom and gather it slightly to produce the ruching effect (see 3); let dry briefly.

5 After you have made 5 petals, it helps to lay them together to check that the sizes all match, before you move on to the next flower. Repeat for the remaining petals, using the appropriate cutter sizes.

6 To make the leaves, use the medium-size circle cutter and roll out petal shapes as before.

7 To shape the leaves, fold over the two sides at the top half of the circle to a tip and pinch lightly. Gather and pinch the paste together at the bottom to a leaf shape (see 4).

8 For the flower centers, shape small balls of paste about ¼ inch in diameter.

9 Spray all flower petals, leaves, and flower centers evenly with pearl luster spray. Alternatively, you can brush them individually with luster dust, but it takes much longer (see 5).

TO ASSEMBLE AND FINISH

10 Spread a small amount of royal icing in the middle of the iced cake board and place the cake on top.

11 Secure the white ribbon around the bottom of the cake and the iced cake board with blobs of royal icing.

12 In a small bowl, mix the remaining royal icing with a little water to soft-peak consistency (page 132) and put into a pastry bag.

13 Snip a small tip off the bag and pipe a row of fine dots around the ribbon edges at ½-inch intervals.

14 Place the cake on the turntable and tilt it slightly away from you. Start decorating it by piping swirls all around the sides and the top.

15 Finally, stick on the flowers and leaves using royal icing (see 6).

**MAKES ABOUT 170 FINGER-SIZE PORTIONS OR
75 DESSERT PORTIONS**

Summer symphony

Inspired by Neapolitan ice cream, I designed this cake for a summer
wedding, but it suits any summer party. The decoration is fairly simple, so
it is a relatively easy cake to make for larger numbers. Try making it with
different layers of vanilla, pistachio, strawberry, and chocolate filling.

INGREDIENTS

4-inch round cake, made from ¼
recipe quantity Victoria Sponge
Cake, flavored to your choice
(page 114), covered with 14
ounces each marzipan and pastel
pink rolled fondant (page 125–6)

6-inch round cake, made from ½
recipe quantity Victoria Sponge
Cake as above, covered with 1¼
pounds each marzipan and
pistachio-colored rolled fondant

8-inch round cake, made from 1
recipe quantity Victoria Sponge
Cake as above, covered with 1¾
pounds each marzipan and ivory-
colored rolled fondant

10-inch square cake, made from 2
recipe quantities Victoria Sponge
Cake, covered with 2¾ pounds
each marzipan and pistachio-
colored rolled fondant

scant 1½ cups Royal Icing (page
132)

ivory, pink, and moss green food
colors
about 9 ounces white rolled
fondant
small amount of gum tragacanth
small amount of vegetable
shortening
edible glue or alcohol

TOOLS

12 plastic dowels
13-inch square cake board, covered
with about 2 pounds pastel pink
sugar paste (page 125-6)
8-inch cake board for use as a
template
several paper pastry bags (page 134)
1¼ yards ivory satin ribbon, ³/₈-inch
wide
tilting turntable
small rolling pin
confectioners' sugar for dusting
small lattice–impression rolling pin
round pastry cutter, about 1½-
inches diameter

small round pastry cutter, about
¼-inch diameter
about 1½ yards Neapolitan striped
ribbon, 1-inch wide
about 1¾ yards Neapolitan striped
ribbon, 1½-inches wide
about 1½ yards pastel pink satin
ribbon, ³/₈-inch wide
about 1²/₃ yards pastel pink satin
ribbon, about ¼-inch wide
double-sided sticky tape

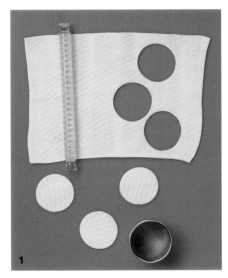

1

2

3

1 Using the template on page 144, mark positions for dowels on all but the smallest cake. Push 4 dowels into place on each of the 3 cakes as described on page 128.

2 Spread a thin layer of icing in the middle of the iced cake board and place the 10-inch square tier on it.

3 Now spread a little icing in the middle of the top of that tier and place the 8-inch ivory tier on top; let set for about half an hour.

4 While it dries, using the 8-inch cake board as a guide, centered on top of the second tier, scratch a circle. Then poke tiny holes along this line at ½-inch intervals; this indicates where to pipe stripes.

5 Prepare pastry bags for piping the stripes: one with pastel pink and another with pistachio green soft-peak royal icing (page 132).

6 Place the ivory ribbon around the bottom of the second tier and secure the ends with icing at the back.

7 Place the stacked tiers on the turntable and slightly tilt away from you. Pipe green lines down the side, starting at the little holes and moving the bag straight down, finishing with a small dot (see 3).

8 Pipe a pastel pink stripe in between every other green one, finishing in the same way with a small dot at the bottom; let dry.

9 For the third tier, mix about 7 ounces rolled fondant with a little ivory color and gum tragacanth. Place the fondant on a lightly greased plastic board and roll out about ⅛ inch thick.

10 For the wafer-effect pattern, roll over the paste once with the lattice-embossed rolling pin, keeping the pressure the same at all times.

11 Using the largest cutter, cut out discs (see 1) and stick them evenly around the cake, using edible glue. Put the third tier in place on top of the second, fixing it with icing.

12 For the top tier, divide the remaining fondant into 3, keep one ivory and mix the other two with pink food color to make one light pink and the other dark pink.

13 Roll all colors of paste out to about 1/16 inch thick and cut out little dots using the smallest circle cutter (see 2). Stick randomly all over the top tier, using edible glue or clear alcohol.

14 Place the narrow Neapolitan ribbon around the base of the bottom tier and secure with icing. Do the same with the wider pastel pink ribbon on the cake board.

15 Put the top tier in position on the third tier, securing it with royal icing. Place the narrower pastel pink ribbon around the base of the top tier, sticking it in place with icing.

16 Tie the wider Neapolitan ribbon into a bow and, using icing, stick it on the side of the top tier, resting on the third tier. Snip the ribbon tails in a V-shape.

pink *Poodles*

Fun and flirtatious, this cake provides the perfect opportunity to send a message of love! It's not just a great design for a loved one's birthday, but simply by rewording the message you can also turn it into a great gift for a couple's wedding anniversary or engagement party.

INGREDIENTS

3 square cake tiers of 4, 6, and 8 inches, made of a cake and filling of your choice (pages 114-21), covered with marzipan and ivory rolled fondant, stacked and assembled on a 12-inch square cake board (pages 128-9)

about 1¼ cups Royal Icing (page 132)

burgundy and black food paste colours

small amount of vegetable shortening

about 10 ounces white gum paste

small amount of edible glue

TOOLS

spatula

small bowls

plastic acetate sleeve

poodle and Eiffel Tower templates (page 144)

plastic wrap or resealable plastic bag

small nonstick plastic board

waxed paper

small plastic rolling pin

small kitchen knife

artist's brush

pair of scissors

selection of small heart-shaped cutters

about 4 yards black-and-white microdot satin ribbon, ⅜-inch wide

small piece of double-sided tape

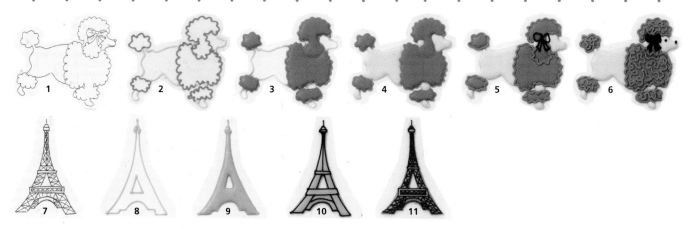

MAKE THE RUN-OUTS AND THE BOW A DAY AHEAD

FOR THE RUN-OUTS

1 Prepare your pastry bags: you will need:

1 bag each soft-peak (page 132) bright pink royal icing (made from burgundy food color) and runny bright pink icing

1 bag each soft-peak pale pink royal icing (made from burgundy food color) and runny pale pink icing

1 bag each gray soft-peak royal icing (made from black food color) and runny gray icing

1 bag each black soft-peak royal icing and black runny icing

2 Rub a very thin layer of shortening over the acetate sleeve. Lay it on top of the poodle template (see 1), greased side up, and pipe the outlines using soft-peak pale pink and gray royal icing for the bodies and bright pink and black for fur (see 2).

3 Flood the middles of the fur with the coordinating runny icing colors (see 3); let them dry a little bit. Once the icing is beginning to set you can flood the bodies with the coordinating icing colors (see 4); let dry overnight.

4 For the Eiffel Tower, outline the shape (see 7) with the soft-peak gray icing (see 8) and flood it with the same color of runny icing (see 9); let it dry overnight.

5 Once the run-outs have dried completely, pipe the details of the fur, the bows, and faces on the poodles, as well as the Eiffel Tower structures, using the soft-peak royal icing colors accordingly (see 5, 6, 10 and 11); let the icing dry completely.

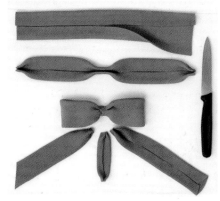

FOR THE BOW

6 Mix the gum paste with the burgundy food color and a small amount of shortening to a bright pink smooth and pliable paste. Keep it covered with plastic wrap or inside a resealable plastic bag to prevent it from drying out.

7 Take about half of the paste and roll it out on a slightly greased non-stick plastic board to about 1/8 inch, 4 inches wide and 10 inches long.

8 Trim the edges with a knife and fold each side of the paste horizontally toward the middle (see left). Pinch the strip of paste together in the middle as well as on both ends. Brush a small amount of edible glue into the middle of the paste, fold both ends over and pinch them down in the middle.

9 For the middle part of the bow roll out a smaller piece of paste to the same thickness as before and about 1¾ inches wide by 3¼ inches long. Fold it as before and pinch both ends together.

10 Brush a thin layer of edible glue on both ends and wrap the strip around the middle of the bow. Let the bow dry. Keep the leftover pink paste wrapped until the next day.

11 Use the soft-peak black icing to pipe your inscription on the front of the middle tier. If you have good practice in piping free-hand then use your own free-hand style. If you are a bit nervous about this, however, then simply first trace the message onto waxed paper and, using it as a template, scratch it into the icing with a scriber needle. If you tilt the cake away from you slightly, it is easier to follow the marks with your pastry bag.

12 Cut the ribbon into 4 pieces long enough to fit around the individual tiers and the cake board. Secure the ribbon around the cake tiers with dabs of royal icing, and the ribbon on the board with double-sided tape.

13 Make sure the run-outs are completely dry. Using a spatula, carefully lift the poodle and Eiffel Tower run-outs off the cellophane. Using a little royal icing, stick the poodles on the front of the bottom tier, facing each other, and the Eiffel Tower on the top tier.

14 Before sticking the bow on top of the cake, make the bow tails by repeating step 8. Once folded, cut the strip of paste in half and pinch each tail on one end, and cut it at an angle on the other end (see opposite page).

15 Brush the middle of the top tier and the two front corners with edible glue, then stick the tails on so they are falling over the corners toward the front of the cake.

16 Now stick the bow on top, where the tails join, securing it with edible glue.

17 Roll the leftover pink paste out to about $1/16$ inch thick and cut out little heart shapes. Stick them all over the cake as shown.

Anemone
cake

Anemones look great for any vintage-themed party, be it a birthday,
a mother's day lunch, or a wedding. The original idea for this design
comes from a cake I created for the style pages of *Wedding Magazine* in
the UK. The black-and-cream color combination is very contemporary, yet
the frilly petals with a hint of dusky pink add a touch of romance.

INGREDIENTS

one 6-inch round cake with flavor and
  filling of your choice (pages 114-
  21), covered with marzipan and
  ivory rolled fondant (pages 125-6)
  on an ivory-iced 8-inch round cake
  board (page 127)
about 5 ounces white gum paste
ivory and black food color pastes
small amount of vegetable shortening
small amount of cornstarch for dusting
small amount of black sprinkling sugar
edible dusky pink blossom dust
small amount of Royal Icing (page 132)

TOOLS

small nonstick plastic board
small rolling pin
anemone petal cutters (small, medium,
  and large)
flower foam pad
Stayfresh multi-mat
ball tool
veining tool
plastic paint palette
edible glue
fine artist's brush
plastic wrap or resealable plastic bag
small scissors
black flower stamen
paper pastry bags (page 135)
20-inch black-and-white microdot
  ribbon, 1-inch wide
26 inches black-and-white microdot
  ribbon, ⅜-inch wide
double-sided tape
about 20 inches cream-colored satin
  ribbon, 1¼-inch wide

1 Mix 4 ounces white gum paste with a small amount of ivory food color and a dab of shortening into a smooth and pliable paste.

2 On a lightly greased plastic board, roll out the paste 1/16 to 1/8 inch thick. Cut out petal shapes using the anemone petal cutters (see 1). For the 2 large flowers you need 4 large and 4 medium petals each; for the small flower, 4 medium and 4 small petals.

3 Place a couple of petals on the flower foam pad at a time, keeping the others covered with the multi-mat. Flatten each petal with the ball tool and slightly frill the edges (see 2).

4 Roll the veining tool lengthwise across each petal to emboss the veins (see 3). Once they are all shaped, leave them to set slightly in the wells of the paint palette.

5 Once feeling slightly rubbery, stick together the 4 larger petals, using a small amount of edible glue at the bottom tips, and place inside a well of the palette that has been lightly dusted with cornstarch (see 4 and 5.)

6 Stick the 4 smaller petals on top of the large, using the edible glue.

7 To make the flower middles, mix the remaining gum paste to black

and roll into 2 hazelnut-size balls and one slightly smaller.

8 While the balls are still soft, cut the black stamens slightly longer than 1/2 inch (see 6). Dip the bottom part into the glue and push them into the sides of the balls to create an even ring of stamens (see 7).

9 Brush the tops of the black balls with edible glue and dip them upside down into the black sprinkling sugar to give them a bit of texture (see 8).

10 Now stick each flower center into the middle of each anemone using a small amount of edible glue and let it dry completely.

11 Once dry, brush the petal tips of the anemones with the dusky pink blossom dust (see 9).

12 Prepare 2 bags of royal icing; one filled with ivory stiff-peak, and the other with black soft-peak icing. (page 132)

13 Arrange the cream satin ribbon around the base of the cake and stick it with ivory icing, followed by the 1-inch black-and-white ribbon. Tie a little bow out of the remaining black-and-white 1-inch ribbon and stick it on the side of the cake with the double-sided tape. Then arrange the 3/8-inch ribbon around the cake board and secure it with double-sided tape.

14 Pipe small dots evenly all over the cake using black icing. Stick the anemones in a cluster on the edge of the cake using the ivory icing.

Mochaccino dots

This is a simple but smart idea for a truly scrumptious dessert cake to have with a cup of coffee! The polka dots don't just look fun and are easy to make, but they are also very helpful when dividing the cake into perfect portions—one dot for a cocktail-size party portion, two dots for dessert.

INGREDIENTS

1 Rich Dark Chocolate Cake baked one day in advance (pages 115-6) in a rectangular baking tray about 15 x 12 inches (you can use a smaller tray that fits your oven)

1 cup Vanilla Buttercream (page 120)

2 cups Mocha Buttercream (page 120)

about 7 ounces Ganache (page 121)

about 1¼ pounds chocolate covering paste

about 10 ounces ivory rolled fondant

dark brown food paste color

confectioners' sugar, for dusting

small amount of clear alcohol or edible glue

TOOLS

cake leveler

spatula

knife

pastry brush

rolling pin

round pastry cutter, about 1½ inches

plastic wrap

microwave

1 Cut the rich dark chocolate sponge horizontally in half and trim the top and bottom crusts, using the cake leveler. Slice each piece of cake into 2 even layers, using the cake leveler.

2 Sandwich the 4 layers together, with alternating layers of mocha and vanilla buttercream.

3 Once all the layers are stacked together, wrap the cake in plastic wrap and chill until it sets and feels firm. This can take a few hours, depending on your refrigerator.

4 Once the cake is set, prepare the chocolate covering paste. It is usually firm when cold and needs to be softened in the microwave at medium heat about 5 seconds.

5 Knead the paste until pliable. Roll it out on a surface dusted with confectioners' sugar to a thickness of about ¼ inch and large enough to cover the cake's top.

6 Remove the cake from the refrigerator and spread the top with a very thin layer of ganache.

7 Place the sheet of paste on top and trim the excess off the sides.

8 Using a sharp knife, trim a thin slice off all the sides of the cake to give it a perfect, clean shape.

9 Divide the ivory fondant into 3 portions and mix each one with a different small amount of the leftover chocolate covering paste until you end up with café latte-, caramel-, and mocha-colored pieces of fondant.

10 On a flat surface dusted with confectioners' sugar, roll out each piece of fondant until about ⅛ inch thick. Cut out enough dots to cover the top of the cake.

11 Brush the back of each dot with a little clear alcohol or glue and arrange them in rows, alternating colors.

couture *Hatboxes*

Ever since I moved to London and discovered the British designer Lulu Guinness's fabulous designs, I have been fascinated by hatboxes, in particular stripy ones with pretty bows. I thought these could be a fun and quirky idea for a girly birthday cake and a rather more special alternative to a gift box cake.

INGREDIENTS

Two 6-inch hexagonal cakes with the filling of your choice (pages 113-8), covered with marzipan and one with lilac rolled fondant and the other with dusky pink (pages 125-6) rolled fondant (the quantities needed for a hexagonal cake work out to be the same as for a round cake)

One 9-inch hexagonal cake with the filling of your choice, covered with marzipan and purple rolled fondant

about 7 ounces ready-to-use white rolled fondant

about 10 ounces white gum paste

small amount of vegetable shortening

purple, dusky pink, and ivory food paste colours

edible glue

iced-coffee luster dust

small amount of Royal Icing (page 132)

TOOLS

small nonstick plastic board

small rolling pin

plastic wrap or resealable plastic bag

small knife

Stayfresh multi-mat

fine artist's brush

4 plastic dowels

Serrated knife

dowels template (page 144)

edible marker pen

design wheeler

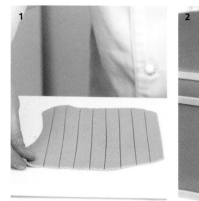

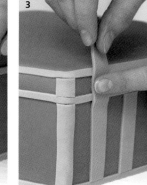
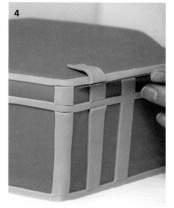

1 Mix the rolled fondant and the gum paste together with a small amount of shortening to make a smooth and pliable modeling paste.

TIP: To create a soft and smooth modeling paste, I mix rolled fondant with gum paste. The ratio required depends on how strong it needs to be—the more gum paste the stronger the paste. In general, I use a ratio of equal parts of each or up to two-thirds gum paste to one-third rolled fondant.

2 Divide the mixed paste into 4 equal portions. Mix one with the purple food color to a deep purple shade and one to a lilac, then mix the dusky pink shade and one to a dark cream color, using the ivory food color. Store wrapped in plastic wrap or a resealable plastic bag to prevent them from drying out.

DECORATE ALL CAKE TIERS WITH STRIPS:
3 To make the strips for the purple cake, roll the dusky pink paste out on the nonstick plastic board until about 1/16 inch thick. Cut out thin strips about 1/4 inch wide and stick

them around the bottom and top edge with edible glue. Place another strip about 1/2 inch below and parallel to the strip at the top. If your strips are not long enough to go all around the cakes, join them on the corners.

4 Now roll out another piece of the paste and cut out more strips about 1/2 inch wide and long enough to cover the depth of the cake (see 1). Keep the ones you aren't working with covered with the multi-mat so they don't dry out.

5 Brush the area of cake that will be covered with paste with edible glue (see 2) and place a fondant paste strip on top (see 3). Trim overlapping paste with a knife (see 4).

6 Continue to arrange the strips all around the sides of the cake with even gaps in between. Next, do the same for the top of the cake.

7 Repeat steps 3 to 6 for the remaining 2 cake tiers, using the purple paste to make the strips for the lilac cake, and the lilac paste to make the strips for the dusky pink cake; let dry until all the strips harden.

STACKING THE 2-TIER CAKE:
8 Dowel the 9-inch bottom tier as described on pages 128-9 and stick the 6-inch lilac cake with the purple strips on top of it with royal icing.

MAKING THE BOWS:
9 For the bow of the large cake, roll the cream-colored modeling paste out to about 1/8 inch thick and cut it into strips about 1 inch wide and 2½ inches long. Mark / emboss a stitched design along both sides of each strip using the design wheeler (see 5). Brush the strips with the iced-coffee luster dust (see 6).

10 Turn one of the strips upside down and pinch the paste together in the middle. Then fold both ends toward the middle and pinch them together, using a small amount of edible glue to hold them in place (see 7).

11 Use another strip of the paste to make the tails. Fold it over in the middle so both tails are facing to one side in a V-shape. Cut the tails at an angle with a knife (see 8).

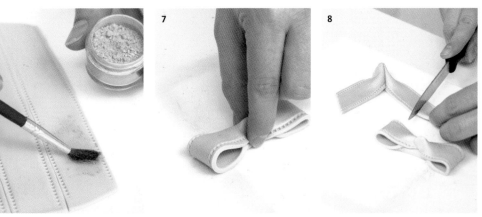

12 Cut a 1¾-inch-long piece off the remaining strip of paste and wrap it around the middle of the bow, using a little edible glue to stick it on.

13 Repeat steps 9 through 12 for the 2 remaining smaller bows, cutting the strips of paste slightly thinner and shorter than before.

14 Let the bows and tails set a little bit, then, once they feel slightly rubbery, stick them on the front of each cake with edible glue.

15 For the handles, roll the rest of the cream colored paste out to the same thickness as before and as long as possible. Cut it into three ¼-inch-wide strips and emboss each with a stitching design along the middle, using the design wheeler; brush with iced-coffee pearl luster.

16 Shape 12 small balls from the trimmings of the cream fondant and brush them with the luster as well.

17 Using the edible glue, attach the box handles to the sides of each box and arrange them on top of each tier. Place a ball at the end of each handle.

coco's *Corsage*

My inspiration here comes from the undisputed doyenne of haute couture Coco Chanel. The lattice design is iconic for so many of her creations and the color combination of navy, cream, and pearl is simply timeless and elegant. This cake suits any sophisticated wedding or other occasion.

INGREDIENTS

2 round cake tiers, 8 inches and 5 inches, flavored to your choice, freshly iced with marzipan and ivory rolled fondant (see pages 114-21 and 125-6)
Pearl Lustre Spray (PME) or luster dust
small quantity Royal Icing (page 132)

TOOLS

turntable (optional)
ruler
scriber tool
design wheeler with stitching attachment
4 plastic dowels
serrated knife
small spatula
3½ yards navy satin ribbon, 2 inches wide
pair of scissors
double-sided tape
pearl diamante brooch
5 or 6 medium-sized cream color roses (not treated with pesticides)

1 While the icing is still soft, using a ruler and a scriber, mark the sides of each tier with a row of dots around the top edge spaced about 1 inch apart. Repeat this around the middle of each tier and around the bottom, making sure the dots all line up underneath each other (see 1).

2 Using the dots as a spacing guide, emboss a diagonal lattice design with the design wheeler all around the sides of both of the tiers (see 2 and 3).

3 Spray the icing all over with a light dusting of pearl shimmer.

4 Dowel the bottom tier as described on pages 128-9. Stick the smallest tier on top with royal icing.

5 Cut the ribbon to fit around the bottom and top tiers, and secure both in place with dabs of icing.

6 Tie a bow out of the remaining piece of ribbon, attach the brooch in the middle of the bow, and stick on to the ribbon at the front of the top tier with double-sided tape.

7 Arrange the roses on top of the cake and sprinkle a few petals around cake table.

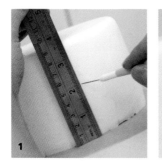

Button
flowers cake

This cool cake for crafty chicks and domestic goddesses was inspired by
a button flower brooch. The cake design is daringly different, almost
whimsical and frivolous.

INGREDIENTS

two 2½-inch-deep cakes, one 4-inch-
square and another 8-inch-square,
flavored and filled to your choice
(pages 114-21), covered with
marzipan and ecru rolled fondant
(pages 125-6)

one 4-inch-deep, 6-inch-square cake,
flavored and filled to your choice,
covered with marzipan and peach-
colored rolled fondant

one 4-inch-deep, 10-inch-square cake,
flavored and filled to your choice,
covered with marzipan and soft
pink-colored rolled fondant

all cakes assembled on a 12-inch-
square cake board covered with
ecru icing (page 127)

about 14 ounces white gum paste

small amount of vegetable shortening

ivory, pink, peach, and dark brown
food colors

pearl luster spray

edible iced-coffee luster dust

small amount of edible glue

small amount of Royal Icing (page 132)

TOOLS

plastic wrap or resealable plastic bag

small nonstick plastic board

small rolling pin

3 round cutters, about ¼, ⅜, and ¾
inch diameter

scriber tool

ordinary rolling pin

linen-look roller

6-petal pastry cutter, about 3¼ inches
diameter

petunia cutter, medium-size

Bridal Lily Cutter (FMM)

fine artist's brush

soft artist's brush for dusting

small and medium arum lily petal
cutter or other simple leaf cutter

small 5-petal cutter, 10-inch diameter

flower foam pad

bone tool

about 3½ yards ecru-colored ribbon
with stitched edges, ½-inch wide

paper pastry bag (page 134)

small spatula

about 1½ yards ecru-colored satin
ribbon, ¾-inch wide

1 Mix the gum paste with a small amount of shortening until smooth and pliable.

2 Divide the modeling paste into 4 equal portions and mix one to an ivory, one to a soft pink, one to a peach, and one to an ecru (using a small amount of dark brown) shade. Keep them covered with plastic wrap or inside a resealable plastic bag to prevent the pastes from drying out.

MAKE THE BUTTONS: YOU WILL NEED ABOUT 1 ECRU, 32 IVORY, 32 PEACH, AND 22 PALE PINK BUTTONS IN TOTAL.

3 Using one color of paste at a time, roll a small piece of it out until it is $1/16$ to $1/8$-inch thick.

4 Using the $3/4$-inch round cutter, stamp out the button shapes. Then use the $3/8$-inch round cutter to emboss the button edge (see 1).

5 Make 4 little holes in the middle of the buttons using the scriber (see 1); let dry. Repeat for all the remaining buttons.

6 Once all the buttons are made, spray them with the pearl luster spray to make them shiny.

MAKE THE BUTTON FLOWERS:

7 Using a normal rolling pin, roll out the ivory-colored paste until about $1/8$ inch thick.

8 Now emboss the linen texture into the paste by rolling the linen-look roller once across the paste, using an even pressure.

9 Using the 6-petal cutter, cut out 2 large 6-petal flower shapes (see 2).

10 Reroll the ivory trimmings, but using the plain rolling pin, to about $1/16$ inch thick. Use the petunia cutter to cut out 3 petunia shapes (see 6).

11 Now roll out the pale pink paste to the same thickness as before and use the lily cutter to cut out a pale pink lily shape. Repeat for the peach lily using peach-colored paste. Emboss each one with a polka dot pattern, using the $1/4$-inch round cutter (see 3).

12 Roll out the ecru-color paste and cut out 2 more lily flower shapes. Brush them with the iced-coffee luster for a light shimmer and cut out polka dots using the $1/4$-inch round cutter at the same positions of the petals as you embossed the pale

pink and peach lilies (see 4). This makes sure that the dots match perfectly with the edges of the flower petals.

13 Using a fine artist's brush with some edible glue, stick the shimmered dots on the matching embossed dots of the petals of the pale pink and peach lilies.

14 Reroll the remaining ecru-colored paste and cut out 4 medium and 2 small arum lily petals (or leaves, if using leaf cutters), then pinch them to form leaf shapes. Brush with the iced-coffee pearl luster (see 5).

15 To make small 5-petal flower shapes, roll out the peach-colored paste and cut out 2 blossoms. Place on a flower foam pad and slightly stretch each petal with the bone tool (see 7).

16 To assemble the 2 large button flowers, stick the flower shapes on top of each other in the following order, starting with the largest flower on the bottom:
6-petal linen-textured flowers
pink spotty lily flower

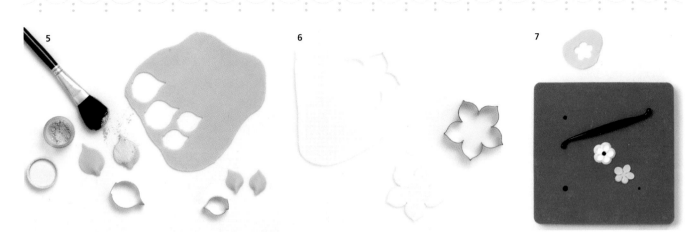

5　　　　　6　　　　　7

small peach 5-petal flower buttons (1 ecru / 1 pink)

For the smaller flower, starting at the bottom:
　ivory petunia flower
　peach 5-petal flower
　pink button

Leave the flowers and leaves to dry.

17 Mix a small amount of royal icing with the dark brown food color and a small amount of water to an ecru color soft-peak royal icing consistency (page 132).

18 Arrange the stitched ribbon around the bottom of each tier and secure in place with dabs of icing. Arrange the plain ribbon around the cake board in the same way.

19 Stick the buttons on top the ribbons with icing, using the ivory ones for the ecru cake tiers, the pink buttons for the peach tier, and the peach buttons for the pink cake tier.

20 Once flowers and leaves are dry, stick them on the cake with icing.

21 Pipe little crosses into the middle of each button to look like threads.

**MAKES ABOUT 100 FINGER-SIZE
PORTIONS OR 60 DESSERT PORTIONS**

Tiffany pearls

Diamonds may be most girls' best friends, but mine are pearls! And just as much as I like wearing them, I think they look exquisite if iced onto a cake. The piped pearl designs of this cake use a very simple technique, but, yet, they transform a simple cake into a glamorous but understated centerpiece. The individual pearl designs are all inspired by different pieces of jewelry—the band of pearls around the shallower tiers reminds of a choker, the tear droplets of the third tier are taken from a beautiful pair of earrings, and the drapes of the bottom tier originate from a pearl necklace my mom gave to me when I got married.

INGREDIENTS

2 round cake tiers about 4-inches-deep, one 10 inches in diameter and the other 6 inches in diameter

2 round cake tiers about 2½-inches-deep, one 8 inches and the other 4 inches in diameter

all four made of the cake and filling of your choice (pages 114-21), iced with marzipan and pale blue rolled fondant (pages 125-6) with the bottom of the third tier already doweled (pages 127-8)

13-inch round cake board, also iced with pale blue rolled fondant (page 127)

scant 1 cup Royal Icing (page 132)

ivory food paste color

small amount of water

small amount of piping gel

edible pearl luster dust

TOOLS

side scribing / marking gauge

ruler

scriber tool

small spatula

paper pastry bag (page 134)

turntable

fine artist's brush

scissors

about 3 yards bridal white satin ribbon, ¼-inch wide and 1½ yards, ³⁄₈-inch wide

double-sided tape

1

2

3

MARK THE TIERS BEFORE PIPING THE PEARL DESIGNS

1 For the second and top tier, using the side scribing / marking gauge, scribe 3 parallel lines centered along the sides of each tier, spacing them about ½ inch apart.

2 For the third tier scribe a line around the side about 1 inch down from the top edge of the cake (see 1) and divide the line into 12 equal sections, marking them with the scriber. Next, mark the positions for the tear droplets about 2 inches down from each section and again mark them using the ruler and scriber (see 2).

3 For the bottom tier, divide the top edge into 8 even sections and mark these with the scriber.

Now place a ruler centered between each section and mark it at about 1½ inches down from the top edge and another 2 farther down the cake, spacing them about ¾ inch apart from each other. These indicate the lowest points of each of the swags.

PIPE THE PEARL DESIGNS

4 Spread a thin layer of royal icing on the iced cake board and place the bottom tier on top.

5 Mix the remaining royal icing with a little bit of ivory food color and water to a soft-peak off-white color (page 132). Put it in a pastry bag and snip a small tip off the point.

6 One by one, place each tier on top of a turntable and pipe the

pearls, droplets, and swag designs around the sides, using the lines and markings as a guide; let dry.

7 Once dry, mix a small amount of piping gel with a bit of pearl luster dust to a thick paste. Using the artist brush, paint the pearls with the luster to make them shiny (see 3).

8 Stack the tiers on top of one another as described on pages 128-9 and arrange the ¼-inch ribbon around the side of each tier. Secure the ribbons with a dab of royal icing.

9 Arrange the ¾-inch ribbon around the board and stick it down with double-sided tape.

Basics

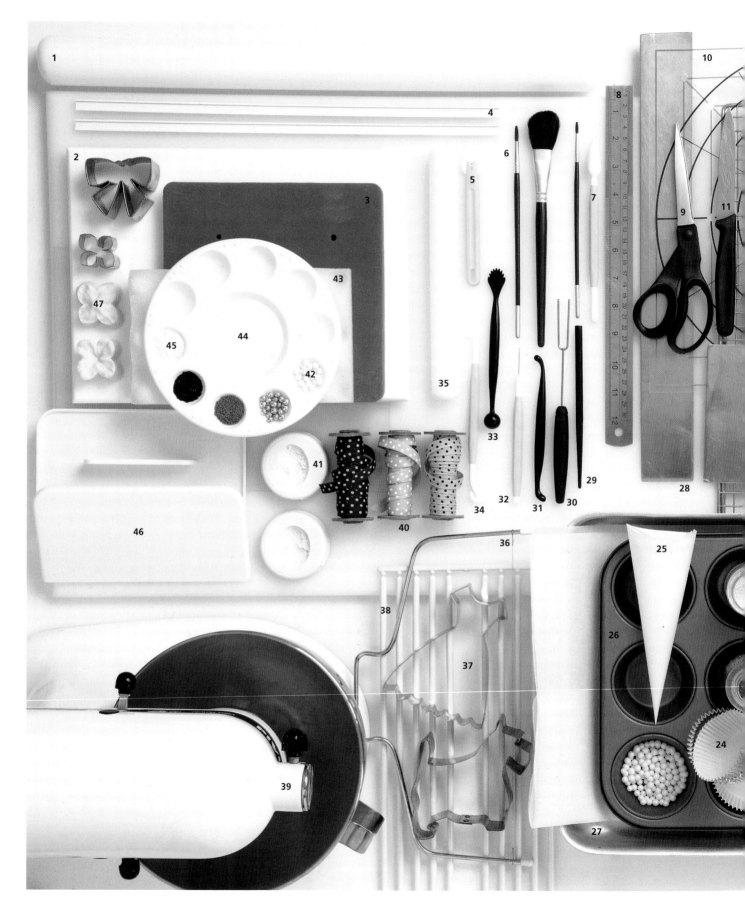

basic tools

1 large rolling pin
2 small nonstick plastic board
3 flower foam pad
4 marzipan spacers
5 design wheeler
6 artists' paint brushes
7 frilling tool
8 ruler
9 scissors
10 dowelling template
11 small kitchen knife
12 small and large spatula
13 large serrated kitchen knife
14 round pastry cutters
15 wire cooling rack
16 assortment of cake boards
17 whisk
18 rubber spatula
19 acetate sheet
20 pastry brush
21 waxed paper
22 cake pans
23 selection of food colors
24 paper muffin cases
25 paper pastry bags
26 muffin tray
27 baking tray
28 metal top and side scraper
29 veining tool
30 truffle dipping fork
31 bone tool
32 scriber needle
33 ball tool
34 cutting wheel
35 small rolling pin
36 cake leveler
37 assortment of cookie cutters
38 plastic dowels
39 mixing bowl / electric mixer with paddle attachment
40 assorted ribbons
41 rubber cameo molds
42 sugar pearls
43 egg crate foam
44 small painter's palette
45 selection of sprinkling sugars
46 cake smoothers
47 hydrangea flower cutter and veiner

food *Colors*

There are basically four different types of food colors used in this book: liquid food colors, paste food colors, blossom tints or dusting colors, and edible luster or Pearl Lustre Spray (PME). Each has its appropriate uses and advantages, and produces a slightly different effect.

LIQUID FOOD COLORS
These usually come in squeeze bottles and are less concentrated. They are perfect for coloring liquid fondant or runny royal icings. Always add the color before adding more liquid to your fondant or royal icings, as it can change the consistency.

PASTE FOOD COLORS
Sold in jars, paste color is perfect for coloring royal icing for piping and sugar paste or gum paste. As it is very concentrated, you will only need a small amount to achieve the required color. Always mix the color to a slightly lighter shade than you are aiming for as it usually darkens slightly once dry.

BLOSSOM TINTS/DUSTING COLORS
These come in jars and are used for brushing gum flower petals and other sugar decorations. They are applied in their dry versions using an artist's brush. They can also be mixed with a small amount of water to create a liquid paint.

EDIBLE LUSTER/PEARL LUSTRE SPRAY (PME)
These are powders or sprays that impart a beautiful satiny shimmer. The powder can be brushed onto the sugar decorations or icing either dry or mixed with clear alcohol or piping gel to create a paint.

baking *Cookies*

The recipes for cookies and cakes that I have developed during the past couple of years produce results that not only taste delicious, but also have a very good texture, and—although light—are solid enough to provide an ideal base for decoration. It is important that you follow each recipe carefully, as baking requires time and patience. As important as it is to master the techniques, it is equally important to use only the best ingredients available, such as organic butter and eggs, real vanilla extract, and high-quality preserves and liqueurs.

MAKES ABOUT 25 MEDIUM OR 12 LARGE COOKIES

sugar *Cookies*

Baking temperature: 350°F;
baking time: 6 to 10 minutes,
   depending on size

INGREDIENTS
1¾ sticks unsalted butter, softened
1 cup sugar
1 large egg, lightly beaten
3 cups all-purpose flour, plus more
   for dusting

OPTIONAL FLAVORS
for vanilla cookies, add seeds from
   1 vanilla bean
for lemon cookies, add finely grated
   zest of 1 lemon.
for orange cookies, add finely
   grated zest of 1 orange.

for chocolate cookies, replace ⅓ cup
   of the all-purpose flour with
   ½ cup unsweetened cocoa powder

TOOLS
electric mixer with paddle
attachment
plastic wrap
pair of marzipan spacers
large rolling pin
cookie cutters in appropriate shapes
small spatula
cookie sheet
waxed paper
wire rack

1 In the electric mixer with paddle attachment, cream the butter, sugar, and chosen flavoring until well mixed and just becoming creamy in texture. Don't overwork, or the cookies will spread during baking.

2 Beat in the egg until well combined. Add the flour and mix on low speed until a dough forms (see 1). Gather it into a ball, wrap it in plastic wrap and chill it at least 1 hour.

3 Place the dough on a floured surface and knead it briefly. Using two marzipan spacers, roll it out to an even thickness (see 2).

1

– 2

3

4 Use cookie cutters to cut out the desired shapes (see 3) and, using a spatula, transfer these on a cookie sheet lined with waxed paper. Chill again about 30 minutes and heat the oven to 350°F.

5 Bake 6 to 10 minutes, depending on size, until golden brown at the edges. Leave to cool on a wire rack. Wrapped in foil or plastic wrap, they will keep well in a cool dry place up to a month.

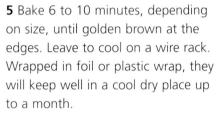

MAKES ABOUT 40 MEDIUM OR 20 LARGE COOKIES

gingerbread *Cookies*

Baking temperature: 400°F;
baking time: 8 to 12 minutes,
    depending on size

INGREDIENTS

5 tablespoons water
1 cup packed brown sugar
3 tablespoons dark molasses or
    treacle
3 tablespoons golden syrup or light
    corn syrup
3 tablespoons ground ginger
3 tablespoons ground cinnamon
1 teaspoon ground cloves
2¼ sticks cold salted butter, diced
1 teaspoon baking soda
4 cups all-purpose flour

TOOLS

deep heavy saucepan
wooden spoon or plastic spatula
electric mixer with paddle
attachment
sifter
plastic wrap
pair of marzipan spacers
rolling pin
assorted cookie cutters
small spatula
cookie sheet
waxed paper
wire cooling rack

GINGERBREAD COOKIES (CONTINUED)

1 Place the water, brown sugar, molasses, golden syrup, ginger, cinnamon, and cloves in a deep, heavy saucepan and bring to a boil, stirring (see 1).

2 Once boiled, remove the pan from the heat and, using a plastic spatula or wooden spoon, carefully stir in the diced butter (see 2).

3 Once these are well combined, add the baking soda and beat the mix through briefly.

4 Pour into the bowl of the electric mixer and leave to cool until just slightly warm.

5 Once the mixture is cool, sift the flour over the top and start combining the two on a low speed, using the paddle attachment, until it forms a wet and sticky dough (see 3).

6 Wrap the dough in plastic wrap and chill a couple of hours or overnight.

7 Place the chilled dough on a floured, clean surface and knead it through briefly.

8 Place the kneaded dough between two ¼-inch guide sticks and roll it out to an even thickness.

9 Use the cookie cutters to cut out the desired shapes and lay them on a cookie sheet lined with waxed paper.

10 Chill again about 30 minutes and heat the oven to 400°F.

11 Bake the cookies in the oven about 8 to 12 minutes, depending on the cookie size, until just firm to the touch.

12 Lift off the tray and leave to cool on a wire rack. Wrapped in foil or plastic wrap, these will keep well in a cool, dry place up to a month.

TIPS

Cookie dough or unbaked cookies can be wrapped in plastic wrap and frozen up to 3 months.

Baked from frozen dough, cookies hold their shape better as they don't tend to spread as much as chilled ones.

Bake equal-size cookies together so they will bake in the same time. If you mix different sizes, the smaller ones will be baked when the larger ones are still raw in the middle.

Baked sugar cookies will keep up to 1 month and gingerbread cookies up to 3 months, if kept in an airtight container or cookie jar.

baking *Cakes*

While traditional Victoria sponge and Rich Dark Chocolate cake are still the most popular choices for large cakes, as well as cup cakes and fondant fancies, I have noticed a growing trend for more adventurous types of cake, such as carrot cake for the more health conscious, or marble cake, because it looks so stunning when sliced. I have also recently widened my repertoire of fillings so my cakes are just as exciting to bite into as they are to look at.

lining *Cake Pans*

1

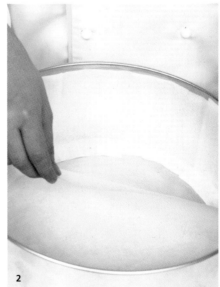

2

TOOLS

square or round cake pan of the
   required size
waxed paper
pencil
pair of scissors

1 Place the cake pan on top of the waxed paper, draw a line around the bottom with a pencil, and use that as a guide to cut out a piece to line the base.

2 Next, cut out a strip that is about 2 inches taller than the sides of your tin and long enough to line the inside edge. Fold 1 inch of this strip over along its length and cut little snips along the folded edge up to the crease.

3 Place the long paper strip with the snipped edge at the bottom inside the pan to cover the sides.

4 Now place the paper liner on top and make sure the snips and the base form a sharp corner and won't allow any dough to leak through the paper lining (see 2). For square pans, use the same technique as above, but fold the long strip that covers the sides at the four corners to fit neatly inside the pan (see 1).

victoria *Sponge cake*

Baking temperature: 350°F;
baking time: 12 to 15 minutes for
cupcakes, 20 to 45 minutes for
large cakes, depending on size

INGREDIENTS

1¾ sticks salted butter, softened

1 cup sugar

4 large eggs

1⅓ cups self-rising flour

6½ tablespoons sugar syrup (page
119), flavored to your choice

TOOLS

electric mixer with a paddle
attachment

mixing bowl

cake pan for large cake, baking tray
for fondant fancies, muffin
trays and muffin cases for
cupcakes

wooden skewer

waxed paper

large spatula for large cakes and
fondant fancies

small spoon or large plastic
pastry bag for cup cakes

wire cooling rack

pastry brush

For other sizes and quantities, refer
to the guide on page 138.

OPTIONAL FLAVORS

For a vanilla cake, add the seeds of
1 vanilla bean

For a lemon cake, add the finely
grated zest of 2 lemons

For an orange cake, add the finely
grated zest of 2 oranges

TIP: I recommend baking cup cakes
on the same day they will be iced,
as they tend to dry out faster than
large cakes.

1 Heat the oven to 350°F.

2 Place the butter, sugar, and
chosen flavoring in the bowl of an
electric mixer and, using the paddle,
cream together until pale and fluffy.

3 Beat the eggs lightly in another
bowl and slowly add to the mix, while
paddling on medium speed. If the mix
starts to look curdled, add a little flour.

4 Once the eggs and the butter
mixture are combined, mix in the
flour at low speed.

5 Line the required baking pan as
explained on the previous page. For

cupcakes, place the paper cases into the muffin trays.

6 Spread the batter evenly into the pan using a spatula (see 1 and 2).

TIP: As a sponge cake always rises more in the middle, spread it slightly higher around the sides. For cupcakes, fill the paper cases about two-thirds full, using a small spoon or a plastic pastry bag.

7 Bake 12 to 15 minutes for cupcakes and 20 to 45 minutes for large cakes, depending on size. The cake is baked when it springs back to the touch and the sides are coming away from the pan.

Alternatively, you can check it by inserting a clean, thin knife into the middle; it should come out clean.

8 Once the cake is baked, let it rest about 15 minutes on a wire rack.

9 Prick the top of the cake with a wooden skewer and, using a pastry brush, soak it with the syrup, while the cake is still warm. For cupcakes, wait about 10 minutes after baking before soaking the cupcakes with the sugar syrup. This way they will absorb the syrup immediately and will not seem dry.

10 Once cool, remove the cake from the pan and cool on wire rack.

11 For large cakes, once cool, wrap them in waxed paper and then foil, and store in a cool, dry place overnight. I prefer to let cakes rest overnight, as they tend to crumble if cut, layered, and iced on the same day of baking.

12 Sponges and cupcakes have a shelf life up to 7 days after icing, and are suitable for freezing. If wrapped well, they can be frozen up to 1 month.

**MAKES ONE 8-INCH CAKE
OR 20 TO 24 CUPCAKES**

rich dark *Chocolate* cake

Baking temperature: 325°F;
baking time: about 15 minutes for cupcakes, 25 to 45 minutes for large cakes, depending on size.

INGREDIENTS

3 ounces dark couverture chocolate, chopped
scant ½ cup milk
heaped packed 1 cup brown sugar
¾ stick salted butter, softened
2 large eggs, slightly beaten
2 cups all-purpose flour

1½ tablespoons unsweetened cocoa powder
½ teaspoon baking powder
½ teaspoon baking soda

TOOLS

cake pans for large cakes or fondant fancies, muffin trays and cases for cupcakes
waxed paper
deep saucepan
electric mixer with paddle attachment
sifter

mixing bowl
measuring cup
rubber spatula or wooden spoon

For other sizes and quantities, please refer to the guide on page 138. This cake is a little bit more moist than most other chocolate cake recipes, but it is also denser and slightly heavier at the same time, which makes it an excellent base for tiered cakes. It has a shelf life of up to 10 days after icing.

1 Heat the oven to 325°F.

2 Line the required baking pan as described on page 113. For cupcakes, place the muffin paper cases into the muffin trays.

3 Place the chocolate, milk, and half of the sugar into a deep saucepan and bring to a boil, while stirring occasionally.

4 Using an electric mixer with a paddle attachment, beat the butter and the remaining sugar until pale and fluffy.

5 Slowly add the eggs.

6 Sift the flour, cocoa powder, baking powder, and baking soda and add to the mixture while mixing at a low speed.

7 While the chocolate mix is still hot, using a measuring cup, slowly pour it into the batter while mixing at low speed (see 1).

8 Once combined (see 2), pour the batter from the bowl directly into the lined pan (see 3). For cupcakes, first transfer the batter into a measuring cup as it is very liquid, and use to fill the paper cases about two-thirds full.

9 Bake 15 minutes for cupcakes, 25 to 45 minutes for large cakes, depending on size. It is baked when it springs back to the touch and the sides are coming away from the pan. Or, insert a clean kitchen knife into the middle; it should come out clean.

10 Once the cake(s) is/are baked, let rest about 15 minutes. Once cool, remove the cake or cupcakes from the pan.

11 For storage, wrap in waxed paper and then in foil and store in a cool, dry place overnight. I let cakes rest overnight as they tend to crumble if baked, cut, layered, and iced on the same day. For cupcakes, I recommend baking on the same day they will be iced, as they tend to dry out faster. This cake is suitable for freezing. Wrapped well it can be frozen up to 3 months.

Carrot cake

Baking temperature: 350°F
baking time: about 20 minutes

INGREDIENTS
6 tablespoons butter
1⅓ cups grated carrots
½ cup chopped toasted hazelnuts
1¼ cups soft light brown sugar
2 extra-large eggs
1⅓ cups all-purpose flour
1½ teaspoons baking powder
½ teaspoon baking soda
1 teaspoon ground cinnamon

TOOLS
grater
bowls
sifter
small saucepan (optional)
electric mixer with paddle
    attachment
rubber spatula or wooden spoon
cake pan the required size and
    shape
wire cooling rack
waxed paper
aluminium foil
kitchen knife

1

2

1 Melt the butter in a saucepan or in a suitable container in the microwave and let it cool.

2 Grate the carrots (see 1), then put with the nuts and sugar in the bowl of an electric mixer. Beat in the eggs at a medium speed, followed by the cool melted butter.

3 Sift the flour, baking powder, baking soda, and cinnamon into the batter and mix at low speed until combined. Pour into the lined pan (see 2).

4 Bake in the preheated oven about 20 minutes. The cake is baked when it springs back to the touch and the

sides are coming away from the pan. Alternatively, insert a clean knife into the middle and it should come out clean.

5 Once the cake is baked, let it rest about 20 minutes before removing it from the pan and leaving it to cool on a wire rack.

6 For storage, wrap the cake in waxed paper, then in foil and store in a cool, dry place overnight. It has a shelf life of 3 to 4 days after icing. This cake is suitable for freezing; wrapped well it can be frozen up to 3 months.

Marble cake

Baking temperature: 350°F;
baking time: 20 to 45 minutes

INGREDIENTS

FOR THE VANILLA BATTER

6½ tablespoons salted butter,
  softened
½ cup sugar
2 large eggs
⅔ cup self-rising flour

FOR THE CHOCOLATE BATTER

6½ tablespoons salted butter,
  softened
½ cup sugar
2 large eggs
½ cup self-rising flour
⅓ cup unsweetened cocoa powder
pinch of baking powder

½ cup vanilla sugar syrup (page 119)

TOOLS

baking pan in required size and shape
waxed paper
electric mixer with paddle attachment
sifter
bowls
rubber spatula or wooden spoon
tablespoon
truffle dipping fork or fork
pastry brush
wire cooling rack

1 Prepare the vanilla batter as for the
Victoria sponge, page 114, steps 1-6.

2 For the chocolate batter, repeat
Victoria Sponge, steps 1-3, then sift

the flour, cocoa powder, and baking
powder together. Add it to the batter
and mix it together at a low speed.

3 Spread the chocolate batter into
the waxed-paper-lined pan,
smoothing with a spatula, then
spread the vanilla batter on top (see 1).

4 Using a tablespoon, fold through
bit by bit (see 2), then run a fork
through for marbling effect (see 3).

5 Bake in the oven 25 to 45 minutes.
Test if the cake is done with a knife,
as in Carrot Cake (previous page).

6 Continue with steps 8–12 of Victoria
Sponge Cake (except cup cakes).

sugar *Syrups*

Roughly the amount needed for an 8-inch layered cake tier, a 12-inch single tier square cake to make 25 fondant fancies, or 20 to 24 cupcakes.

INGREDIENTS

FOR VANILLA SYRUP

5 tablespoons water
⅓ cup sugar
seeds from ½ vanilla bean or 1 teaspoon Madagascan vanilla extract

FOR LEMON SYRUP

5 tablespoons freshly squeezed lemon juice
⅓ cup sugar
1 tablespoons Limoncello liqueur

FOR ORANGE SYRUP

5 tablespoons freshly squeezed orange juice
⅓ cup sugar
1 tablespoon Grand Marnier liqueur

TOOLS

deep saucepan
spatula

1 Place the water or juice and sugar in a deep saucepan and bring to a boil. Remove the pan from the heat and leave to cool.

2 Once cool, stir in the flavorings.

3 Ideally, let the syrup infuse overnight as this brings out the most in the flavors.

4 To store sugar syrup, keep it in an airtight bottle or container inside the refrigerator. It will last for up to 1 month.

Buttercream frosting

Roughly the amount you will need to layer and cover an 8-inch cake tier

INGREDIENTS
2¼ sticks unsalted butter, softened
1¼ cups confectioners' sugar, sifted
pinch of salt

OPTIONAL FLAVORS
For vanilla buttercream (see 4, add the seeds of 1 vanilla bean
For lemon (see 3), add the finely grated zest of 2 lemons
For orange (see 1), add the finely grated zest of 2 oranges
For strawberry (see 2), add 2 tablespoons good strawberry jam and a tiny drop of pink food color
For chocolate (see 5), replace half the buttercream with chocolate ganache (see opposite page)

For mocha buttercream, add a double shot of cool espresso to the chocolate buttercream

TOOLS
electric mixer with a paddle attachment

For other sizes and quantities, please refer to the guide on page 138.

Following a traditional English recipe, I use equal quantities of butter and confectioners' sugar to make my buttercream. The method is very simple and, as it is an egg-free recipe, it has a longer shelf-life than most other buttercreams.

1 Place the butter, confectioners' sugar, salt, and flavoring in the bowl of an electric mixer and, using the paddle attachment, bring the mixture together on low speed. Turn the speed up and beat until light and fluffy.

2 If not using it immediately, store in a sealed container in the refrigerator. Bring it back to room temperature before use. It has a shelf life of up to 2 weeks if refrigerated.

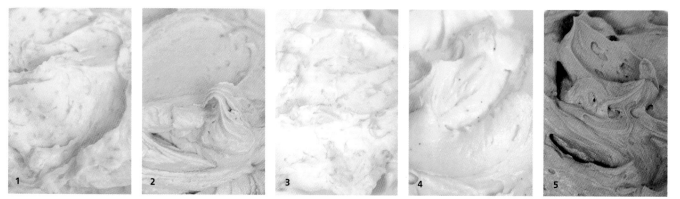

1   2   3   4   5

belgian
Chocolate Ganache

1

3

Roughly the amount you will need to layer and cover an 8-inch cake tier.

INGREDIENTS
18 ounces dark couverture chocolate, chopped, or dark couverture chips (minimum 53% cocoa content)
1¼ cups light cream

TOOLS
heatproof mixing bowl
saucepan
whisk

For other sizes and quantities, please refer to the guide on page 138.

1 Place the chocolate in a bowl and melt in a microwave or over a bain-marie (or bowl set in a roasting pan with hot water coming halfway up the bowl).

2 Place the cream in a saucepan, stir well, and heat to a bare simmer.

3 Pour the hot cream over the chocolate (see 1) and whisk them together, until blended and evenly

colored (see 2 and 3). Don't overwhisk the ganache, as it can break quite easily.

4 Cool slightly until just setting before use. It can be stored in a sealed container in the refrigerator up to a month.

layering and icing *Cakes*

Tiered wedding cakes, as well as miniature cakes, provide the option of mixing different flavors of cakes. If you would like to make a tiered wedding cake with different flavors, you have to bear in mind the bottom tier has to carry the weight of the other tiers and, therefore, a stronger cake base should be used for the bottom tiers with lighter cakes for the top. For example, if you use my recipes, I recommend using chocolate cake for the lower tiers and the lighter Victoria sponge-based cakes for the upper tiers. You will find a full portion guide and charts indicating amounts of basic cake batters, fillings, and covering required for various types and sizes of cakes on page 138. A template for the positioning of dowels to support cake tiers is also given on page 144.

MAKES 8 TO 10 DESSERT-SIZE MINIATURE CAKES

Miniature cakes

I usually bake and layer miniature cakes 3 days in advance, ice them on the next day, and add the decoration one day before the event. The illustrations opposite show a marble cake with buttercream filling but, of course, you can make them with any basic cake and type of filling.

INGREDIENTS

12-inch Square Sponge Cake (page 114)

FOR THE FILLING:

about 4 heaped tablespoons jam, marmalade, lemon curd, buttercream (page 120), or ganache (page 121)

small amount of confectioners' sugar for dusting

about 1¼ pounds buttercream or ganache (pages 120-21), flavored to your choice

3⅓ pounds marzipan

3⅓ pounds white rolled fondant

6½ tablespoons sugar syrup (page 119), flavored to your choice

small amount of clear alcohol (I use vodka as it has a neutral taste) or water

TOOLS

cake leveler or large serrated knife

small spatula

16 thin cake cards to match the size and shape of the cakes (optional)

pastry brush

plastic wrap

large rolling pin

3-inch round high (2-inch) pastry cutter and/or 5 x 3-inch oval cutter

sifter

pair of marzipan spacers

small kitchen knife

pair of cake smoothers

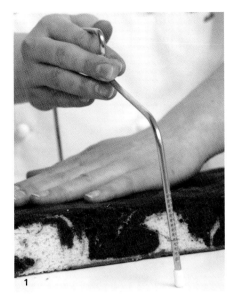

1

2

3

4

5

6

7

8

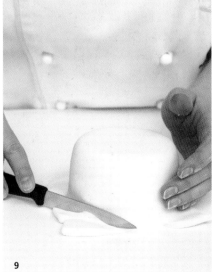

9

1 Using a cake leveler or large serrated knife, trim the top crust off your cake (see 1, previous page).

2 Using the smaller cutters, cut out 16 rounds or 20 ovals from the sheet of sponge (see 2).

3 Place half of them on the cake cards with a dab of buttercream or ganache and soak the tops with sugar syrup (see 3).

4 Using a small spatula, spread them with a layer of the filling of your choice (see 4) and place the other cakes on top of them.

5 Again, soak the tops of the sponges with sugar syrup.

6 Cover each mini cake all around with buttercream or ganache (see 5) and chill until set and feels firm.

7 Once set, on a smooth surface lightly dusted with confectioners' sugar, roll out the marzipan using spacers to get an even thickness. Cut the marzipan into squares that are large enough to cover the cakes.

8 Cover one cake at a time with the marzipan and gently push it down the sides (see 6). Avoid tearing the edges. Trim off the excess using a kitchen knife.

9 Polish the sides and tops of each cake with the cake smoothers (see 7).

10 Let the marzipan set for a few hours, or preferably overnight.

11 Once the marzipan is set, brush each cake with a thin layer of clear alcohol.

12 Repeat steps 7 to 9 (see pics 8 and 9 on the previous page), using the rolled fondant instead of marzipan. Let dry completely, preferably overnight.

MY FAVORITE CAKE AND FILLING COMBINATIONS

• Vanilla sponge cake, soaked with vanilla syrup, layered with raspberry preserves and vanilla buttercream
• Lemon sponge cake, soaked with lemon and Limoncello syrup, layered with lemon curd and lemon buttercream
• Orange sponge cake, soaked with orange and Grand Marnier syrup, layered with luxury orange marmalade and orange buttercream
• Rich dark chocolate cake layered with Belgian chocolate ganache
• Vanilla sponge cake, soaked with morello cherry jam
• Rich dark chocolate cake layered with vanilla buttercream and mocha buttercream
• Vanilla sponge cake layered with vanilla, strawberry, and chocolate buttercream
• Carrot cake layered with lemon buttercream
• Marble cake soaked with vanilla syrup and layered with vanilla buttercream

Large cakes

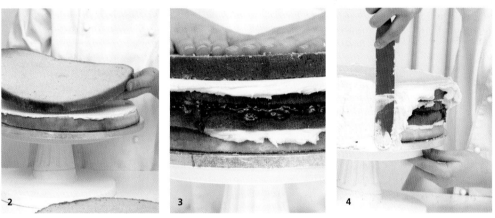

For an 8-inch round cake tier you will need two 8-inch round cakes (see the Quantities Guide on page 138)

INGREDIENTS

about 1¼ pounds buttercream or ganache, or jam, marmalade, or lemon curd (for Victoria Sponge Cake only)

about 1 cup sugar syrup (for Victoria Sponge Cake and Marble Cake only)

confectioners' sugar for dusting

about 2 pounds marzipan

small amount of clear alcohol (I use vodka as it has a neutral taste)

about 1¾ pounds rolled fondant

TOOLS

cake leveler or large serrated knife

small kitchen knife

8-inch round cake board

large spatula

pastry brush

metal side scraper

turntable

sifter

large rolling pin

pair of marzipan spacers

pair of cake smoothers

scriber

1 Using the leveler or serrated knife, trim the top and bottom crusts off both cakes.

2 Slice each cake in half horizontally so you have 4 layers of the same depth (about ¾ inch each).

3 Put the cake board on the turntable and spread it with a thin layer of buttercream or ganache. Place the first sponge layer on top and soak it with the syrup, if required (see 1).

4 Spread the first layer with either buttercream or ganache, place the second layer on top of it (see 2), and soak it again with sugar syrup.

5 Keep on layering the remaining pieces in this way with preserves or buttercream or ganache until all 4 layers are assembled. Press the layers down gently but firmly to make sure that the cake is level (see 3).

6 Using a large spatula, coat the outside of the cake with buttercream or ganache (see 4).

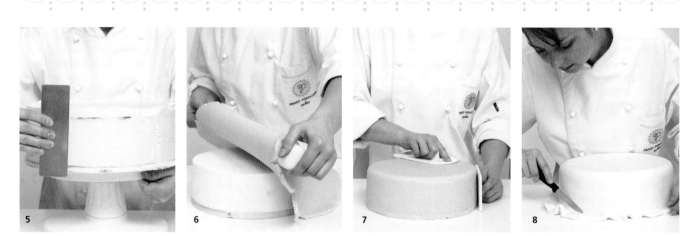

5

6

7

8

Start spreading from the top center and toward the edge as you are rotating the turntable.

7 Push the buttercream down the side and spread it evenly all around the sides.

8 Use a metal side scraper to clean up the sides (see 5) and do the same on the top with the spatula.

9 Chill at least 2 hours, or overnight, until the cake has set and feels firm.

10 Once set, dust a working surface with confectioners' sugar, place the marzipan on top and, using the marzipan spacers, roll out to an even round large enough to cover the top and side.

11 Lift the marzipan with the rolling pin, lay it over the cake (see 6), and gently push it down the sides. Trim off any excess marzipan using the kitchen knife.

12 Polish the marzipan with the cake smoothers (see 7) and use the palms of your hands to smooth the edges. Let the marzipan set, preferably overnight.

13 Once set, brush the marzipan with a thin coat of clear alcohol to stick on the rolled fondant icing. The alcohol not only destroys any bacteria that might have built up while storing the cake, but it also evaporates within minutes after its application and, therefore, creates a strong and hygienic glue between the marzipan and the fondant. (If you prefer not to use alcohol, use boiled cold water instead.)

14 Repeat steps 10 to 12 using rolled fondant instead of marzipan (see 8).

TIPS: for tiered cakes, start the preparation about 5 or 6 days before the event. For example, if the wedding is on a Saturday, bake the cakes on the Monday before and layer them on the Tuesday. Cover the cakes with marzipan on Wednesday and let it set overnight, so it has time to dry. On Thursday, cover the cakes with rolled fondant and let them set again overnight. This gives you the whole of Friday to apply your decorations, which you

can prepare a couple of weeks in advance.

For single tiered cakes, start about 3 to 4 days before the event, as the cake can be covered with marzipan and rolled fondant on the same day. To make one cake tier you need two sponges of the same size.

For a well-proportioned tiered cake, each tier should ideally be about 3½ inches high, including the cake board, before applying the marzipan and icing. Make sure all tiers have the exact same height unless a mixture of different heights is intended.

covering
Cake Boards

1

2

3

Ice your cake board at least 1 or 2 days ahead, to be sure the icing is well set before placing the cake on top.

INGREDIENTS
confectioners' sugar for dusting
small amount of clear alcohol
ready-to-use rolled fondant (see the quantity guide on page 138)

TOOLS
thick cake board of the required size
pastry brush
rolling pin
cake smoother

small kitchen knife
³⁄₈-inch-wide satin ribbon to cover the side
double-sided tape

1 Dust the cake board thinly with confectioners' sugar and brush it with a little alcohol (to make a glue for the rolled fondant).

2 Roll the rolled fondant out to about ⅛ inch thick and large enough to cover the cake board.

3 Using the rolling pin, lift the paste and lay it over the board (see 1).

4 Let the cake smoother glide carefully over the surface of the fondant and push out any air bubbles.

5 Lift the cake board with one hand and push the fondant down the sides with the cake smoother in the other hand (see 2).

6 Trim the excess fondant off with a sharp kitchen knife (see 3) and let the fondant dry 1 to 2 days.

7 Once it is dry, wind the ribbon around the edge of the board and fix the ends with double-sided tape.

assembling *Tiered Cakes*

INGREDIENTS

cake tiers of different sizes, covered
with marzipan and rolled fondant
iced cake board 3 to 4 inches larger
than the bottom tier
Royal Icing (see page 132)
small amount of rolled fondant the
same color as the icing
small amount of water

TOOLS

plastic dowels (4 per tier except the
top one)
large spatula
serrated kitchen knife
pair of strong scissors
food color pen
dowel template (page 144)
paper pastry bag (page 134)
small bowl
damp cloth
level
pair of tweezers

1 Using a large spatula, spread the
middle of the iced board with a thin
layer of icing, making sure it doesn't
exceed the size of the bottom tier.

2 Carefully lift your bottom tier with
the spatula and center it on top of
the cake board (see 1).

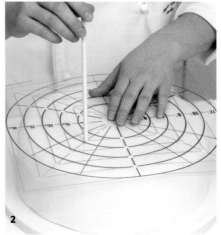

3 Using the template, mark positions
for 4 dowels and push 4 dowels
down into the cake (see 2). (They stop
upper tiers sinking into lower tiers.)

4 With a food color pen, mark each
dowel about $\frac{1}{16}$ inch above the
point where it exits the cake.

5 Carefully remove the dowels, line them up next to one another and cut to the same length, using the average mark as a guide line. Stick them back in the cake. To see if they all have the same height, place a cake board on top of them and check it sits straight, ideally using a small level. If you have to readjust the length of a dowel, carefully pull it out with tweezers and trim with scissors, then replace.

6 Once happy with the dowels, spread a little icing in the middle of the cake, carefully lift the second tier with your spatula and center it on top of the bottom tier.

7 Repeat steps 3 to 6 for the second and third tiers, if required.

8 Once all your tiers are assembled, mix the rolled fondant with water to a thick but smooth paste. Put in a paper pastry bag and squeeze into the gaps between tiers to fill them.

9 Dampen your finger with a damp cloth and run it along the edge to wipe off excess paste.

TIP: Depending on transportation and distance to the event, it can be safer to assemble a tiered cake on site.

MAKES 25 FONDANT FANCIES

dipping *Fondant Fancies*

Liquid fondant icing is widely used as a filling for chocolate truffles, and so on, or as a glaze for pastries. It has a very long shelf life and tastes deliciously smooth when flavored with fruit juices, extracts or liqueurs. As it is white, it provides an ideal base for mixing brilliant colors. Made by boiling together sugar, glucose syrup, and water, it requires experience and skill to achieve the right consistency. To keep it simple, I use ready-made fondant.

INGREDIENTS

8-inch square Victoria Sponge Cake (page 114), well soaked with syrup (page 119), trimmed and layered with the filling of your choice (page 120-21)

1 heaped tablespoon strained apricot jam
confectioners' sugar for dusting
about 5 ounces marzipan
about 2¼ pounds ready-made liquid fondant icing
small amount of liquid glucose
selection of liquid food colors (optional)

TOOLS
tray
plastic wrap
pastry brush
large rolling pin
small knife
microwave
small microwaveable bowls
truffle fork
wire cooling rack

1 Wrap your layered sponge cake in plastic wrap and chill at least 1 hour.

2 Once it is cool and firm, warm the apricot jam, unwrap the cake, and

spread a thin layer of jam over the top, using the pastry brush.

3 On a work surface lightly dusted with confectioners' sugar, knead the marzipan until smooth and pliable. Shape it into a ball and roll it out to a square large enough to cover the top of the sponge and about ⅛ inch thick.

4 Carefully lift it and lay it over the top of the cake. Trim the excess, if necessary.

5 Slice the marzipan-topped sponge into 1¾-inch squares and spread the tops with a thin layer of jam (see 1, previous page) .

6 Put the fondant icing in a large microwaveable bowl and gently heat it in the microwave at medium heat about 1 minute. Stir in the glucose and heat again about 20 seconds at a time, until it is warm and runny.

(Or, heat it in a saucepan over very low heat, stirring. Do not let the fondant boil, or it will lose its shine when cool again.) If necessary, you can add a little sugar syrup to it to make it more liquid. (You are looking for a thick pouring consistency.)

7 If you would like to mix the fondant with different colors, divide it between bowls and add a few drops of food color at a time until you achieve the desired shades.

8 Dip one cake at a time upside down into the fondant (see 2), until about three-quarters of the sides are covered. To lift out, hold with one finger at the bottom and a truffle fork at the top (see 3), making sure you don't push the fork into the marzipan, as it can tear it off. Quickly shake off excess icing and place the cake on the cooling rack (see 4). Leave it for the icing to set.

9 Carefully remove the fancies from the rack by cutting them loose at the bottom using a small kitchen knife, then place in the paper cases, if required. This is best done with slightly wet fingers, to prevent the icing sticking to them. Gently push the sides of the paper case against the sides of the cake and, as they stick, they take on the square shape. Place the cakes closely next to each other until ready for decoration. Again, this will help the paper cases stay square.

10 Iced fondant fancies keep for about 7 days in a cakebox or wrapped in foil. Don't store them in the refrigerator or the icing will melt.

dipping
Cupcakes

INGREDIENTS

2 to 3 tablespoons strained apricot
   jam
20 to 24 well soaked cupcakes
   (page 114)
about 2¼ pounds ready-made liquid
   fondant icing
small amount of plain sugar syrup
1 heaped teaspoon liquid glucose
selection of food colors

TOOLS

pastry brush
microwave
small microwaveable bowls
small spatula

1 Warm the jam and brush a thin layer over each cup cake to seal it (see 1).

2 Put the fondant in a large microwaveable bowl and gently heat in the microwave at medium 1 minute. Stir in the glucose and heat again for 20 seconds at a time, until warm and runny. (Or, heat in a saucepan over very low heat, stirring. Do not let the fondant boil, or it will lose its shine.) If necessary, add a little sugar syrup to make it more liquid. (You are looking for a thick pouring consistency.)

3 If you would like to mix the fondant with different colors, divide it between bowls and add a few drops of color at a time until you get the desired shades.

4 Dip all the cupcakes of one color first into the fondant, shake off excess (see 2) and let set before moving on to the next color. By the time you have dipped the last cakes, the icing of the first will have set and you can begin with the second coat of icing, as before. Dipping each cake twice guarantees a beautifully smooth and shiny surface.

5 Leftover fondant can be stored in a bowl wrapped with plastic wrap. Before using it again, pour some hot water over the top to soften the hardened top and let soak 15 minutes, pour off the water and heat as before.

TIP: Start by mixing lighter fondant shades first and then add more fondant and food color as required. An economic trick is to mix different colored icings to achieve a new color. Say, to make yellow, blue, and green icing, start with yellow in one bowl and blue in another, then mix these together to make green icing.

Royal icing and *Piping*

Piping with royal icing is probably the most essential skill needed for most of my designs, particularly for decorating cookies. Made from confectioners' sugar and either fresh egg white or dried powdered egg white, it also makes an excellent glue for fixing gum paste flowers and other decoration on to cakes. Making royal icing is a very simple procedure; if you find it daunting, however, you can buy ready-made versions from specialty cake decorating suppliers.

MAKES ABOUT 2¾ CUPS

Royal icing

STIFF PEAK CONSISTENCY
For sticking together cake tiers or sticking decorations onto icing.

SOFT PEAK CONSISTENCY
For piping lines, dots, and borders

RUNNY CONSISTENCY
For filling in the middle of spaces

INGREDIENTS

about 1 ounce dry egg white
    powder or whites of 4 large eggs
8⅓ cups confectioners' sugar, sifted
squeeze of lemon juice

TOOLS

sifter
electric mixer with paddle
    attachment
wooden spoon or rubber spatula
sealable plastic container
kitchen cloth

1 If using the dry egg white, mix with water and use as per the pack instructions. Strain to get rid of any lumps. Ideally let this rest overnight in the refrigerator.

2 Place the sugar in the bowl of an electric mixer, add three-quarters of the dry egg white mixture or the lightly beaten egg whites and the lemon juice. Start mixing on low speed.

3 Once well combined, check the consistency. If the sides of the bowl still look dry and crumbly, add some more of the dry egg white mixture or egg white until the icing looks almost smooth but not wet.

4 Keep mixing on slow speed for 4 to 5 minutes, until it reaches stiff-peak consistency.

5 Spoon into a sealable plastic container, and cover with a clean damp kitchen cloth and the lid. Store at room temperature up to 7 days; if using fresh egg, store in the refrigerator. The egg white can separate from the sugar after a couple of days, which will turn the icing into a dry, dense mixture. If this happens, remix at low speed until smooth and at stiff peak consistency again. Make sure no dry icing bits sticking to the sides of your storage container get into the mixing bowl.

ROYAL ICING CONSISTENCIES

Throughout the book, I will refer to the three useful consistencies of royal icing (as opposite), which are important in achieving the right results. Simply thin down your basic royal icing recipe with water, a little bit at a time, using a spatula, until you reach the correct consistency. Always make sure you keep your icing covered with plastic wrap or a damp cloth when not using it, to stop it from drying out.

making a
Paper Pastry Bag

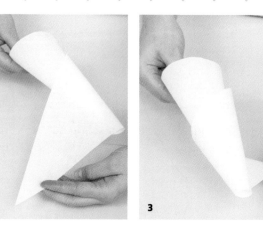

1 Take a rectangular piece of waxed paper, about 12 x 15 inches and cut it from one corner to the opposite one using scissors. Try sliding your scissors through the paper rather than cutting it as this gives a cleaner cut.

2 Hold one of the resulting paper triangles with your hand at the middle of the longest side, and with your other hand on the point on the opposite side. The longer side of the triangle should be on your left and the shorter on the right.

3 Curl the shorter corner on your right over to the corner that is pointing toward you, so it forms a cone (see 1).

4 With your left hand, wrap the longer corner on the left around the tip of the cone twice and join it with the other 2 corners at the back of the cone (see 2 and 3).

5 If the bag still has an open tip at the front, you can close it by wiggling the inner an outer layers of paper back and forth, until the cone forms a sharp point (see 4).

6 Fold the corners at the open end into the inside of the bag twice to form a sturdy edge that will prevent unfurling (see 5).

7 Only ever half-fill the bag or the icing will ooze out when you squeeze. Close by folding the side with the seam over to the plain side twice.

TIP: For extra strength I use "waxed" greaseproof paper, also called "silicon paper", which I buy from a specialty baking supplier.

Piping techniques

The piping techniques demonstrated below are very useful to practise your general piping skills. Instead of piping directly on to a cake, simply take a piece of greaseproof paper and pipe on to that instead. You can also place templates underneath it and trace them through the paper with your piping bag. If you have never piped with royal icing before, this task is a great way to train your skills, after all practice makes perfect.

First snip a small tip off your pastry bag already filled with icing. Hold the bag between the thumb and the fingers of your preferred hand and use the index finger of your other hand to guide the nozzle.

PIPING LINES:

1 Touch the starting point with the tip of the bag and slowly squeeze out the icing. As you are squeezing, lift the bag slightly and pull the line straight toward you or, for example, along the sides of a cookie.

2 Once you are approaching the finishing point, gradually bring the bag down, stop squeezing, and drop the line by touching the finishing point with the tip of the bag.

PIPING DOTS:

1 Hold the tip of your pastry bag about $\frac{1}{16}$ inch above the surface and squeeze out the icing to produce a dot on the surface.

2 Gradually lift the tip as the dot gets larger.

3 Once the dot has reached its desired size, stop squeezing and lift off the tip.

4 If the dot forms a little peak at the top, flatten it carefully with a damp soft artist brush

PIPING LOOPS AND SWAGS:

1 Start as you would for piping lines.

2 Holding your bag at angle of 45° to the surface, touch the starting point with the tip and slowly squeeze out the icing. As you squeeze, lift the bag up by about an inch and pull it from one side to the other in circular movements, overlapping the lines in even intervals to create evenly spaced loops and swags.

TIP: If you find it difficult to space the loops and swags out evenly, mark the points where the loops will meet and use them as guides.

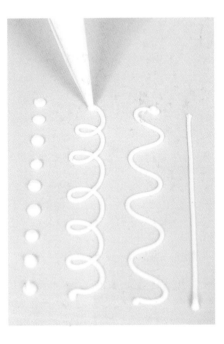

Glossary

Most items are available from specialty suppliers (right), although more everyday ones can be found in supermarkets and cookware stores.

INGREDIENTS

DRIED EGG POWDER This powder is used instead of fresh egg whites in making royal icing for food safety reasons, as the dried egg white is pasteurized.

FONDANT ICING Made from sugar, water, and cream of tartar, fondant is widely used as a glaze in confectionery, as well as in pâtisserie and cake decorating. Ready-made fondant is available as a powder to be mixed with water.

GLUCOSE A thick version of corn syrup used to make fondant icing to give it a beautiful shine.

GUM PASTE A fine and pliable paste made from confectioners' sugar, gelatin, and gum tragacanth, which dries hard, with a porcelain-like texture. It is used to make finely crafted sugar flowers.

GUM TRAGACANTH Made from the dried sap of the Astragalus plant, this is sold as a powdered hardening agent and is mixed with rolled fondant to create a pliable modeling paste for making sugar flowers. It has the additional effect of making the paste set on contact with air. It can also be mixed with a little water to make an edible glue.

LUSTER DUST, EDIBLE This nontoxic pearl dust comes in different shades. It can either be mixed to a thick paste with a drop of alcohol or applied directly with a brush.

MARZIPAN Made from ground almonds and confectioners' sugar, marzipan is used for covering large cakes before icing, as it seals in moisture and helps to stabilize shape. It is also ideal for making flowers, as it is very easy to mold and the individual petals stick to each other naturally.

ROLLED FONDANT A very smooth and pliable icing made from gelatin, confectioners' sugar, and water, which dries hard but is still easy to cut. Rolled fondant is used for covering cakes and for making flowers and modeling cake decorations.

TOOLS

BONE (OR DOG BONE) TOOL A long plastic stick with rounded ends, looking like a bone, this is used to shape rolled fondant petals.

CAKE SMOOTHERS These are flat rectangular pieces of smooth plastic, with a handle, used to smooth the marzipan and rolled fondant on a cake.

DESIGN WHEELER A plastic sugar craft tool with 3 interchangeable heads for creating patterns and designs, such as stitching, on rolled fondant cakes.

DRESDEN TOOL A tool for fluting petals. Its pointed tip is used to emphasize the middle of some flowers and the veining end to make vein markings difficult to create with other veiners.

FOAM PETAL PAD This is used as a yielding surface for thinning the edges of flowers with a bone tool (above).

FLOWER CUTTERS Made of metal or plastic, flower cutters are used to cut petals and leaves out of gum paste. In this book I have used cutters to make roses, petunias, primroses, and violets.

FLOWER STAMEN Similar to the stamen used for silk flowers, these contain small wires and are used for sugar flower middles, although they are NOT edible.

LINEN-LOOK ROLLING PIN A plastic rolling pin with a textured surface that embosses a linen effect into rolled fondant.

MARZIPAN SPACERS Long sticks used to roll out dough, rolled fondant, or marzipan to an even thickness.

PETAL/LEAF VEINING MAT A rubber mat used for shaping and making leaves and petals.

EGG CRATE FOAM A sheet of textured packaging foam with wells (similar to an egg box); useful to support the shape of sugar flowers and leaves when drying.

SCRIBER TOOL A fine metal pin used to mark or scratch designs and patterns into icing.

SIDE SCRAPER Flat piece of metal (ideally stainless steel) with a straight side used for scraping excess cream off the side of a cake's side.

STAYFRESH MULTI-MAT Thick acetate mat used to cover rolled-out rolled fondant to prevent from drying out.

Suppliers

FOR CAKE DECORATING TOOLS, FOOD COLORS, AND GENERAL EQUIPMENT:

USA & CANADA

Bakers Nook
901 W Michigan Ave.
Saline, MI 48176
www.shopbakersnook.com

Cakes by Sam, Inc.
2401 West Highway 89
Cabot, AR 72023
www.cakesbysam.com

Creative Cutters
561 Edward Avenue, Unit 2
Richmond Hill, Ontario
Canada L4C 9W6
1-905-883-5638
www.creativecutters.com

Global Sugar Art
28 Plattsburgh Plaza
Plattsburgh, NY 12901
tel 1-518-561-3039
www.globalsugarart.com

Kitchen Krafts, Inc.
PO Box 442
Waukon, IA 52172
www.kitchenkrafts.com

Sugarcraft, Inc.
2715 Dixie Hwy.
Hamilton, OH 45015
www.sugarcraft.com

Wilton
2240 W. 75th St.
Woodridge, IL 60517
www.wilton.com

FOR COOKIE CUTTERS:

CopperGifts.com
900 N. 32nd St
Parsons, KS 67357
www.coppergifts.com

Kitchen Collectables, Inc.
8901 J. Street, Suite 2
Omaha, NE 68127
www.kitchengifts.com

UK

Almond Art
Unit 15 & 16 Faraday Close
Gorse Lane Industrial Estate
Clacton-on-Sea, Essex
CO15 4TR
01255 223322
www.almondart.com

Jane Asher Party Cakes
24 Cale Street
London SW3 3QU
www.jane-asher.co.uk

Squires Shop and School
Squires House
3 Waverley Lane
Farnham, Surrey
GU9 8BB
www.squires-group.co.uk

FOR FLOWER CUTTERS, VEINERS, AND CAMEO MOLDS:
Design A Cake
30–31 Phoenix Road
Crowther Industrial Estate
Washington,
Tyne & Wear
NE38 0AD
www.design-a-cake.co.uk

ASIA

International Centre of Cake Artistry Sdn. Bhd.
1-1 to 1-3A, Jalan PJU 5/15
Dataran Sunway
Kota Damansara
47810 Petaling Jaya,
Selangor, Malaysia
tel 603 6140 8835
www.2decoratecakes.com

PEGGY PORSCHEN®
cakes

For cake decorating classes and specialist equipment:
For more information on Peggy Porschen's cookies and cakes, or to place an order, please visit her Web site
www.peggyporschen.com

Quantity guides

CAKE BATTER QUANTITY, AND PORTION GUIDE

This chart gives an overview of what size cake you need for your number of guests and the approximate quantity of cake batter needed for the different sizes of cake pans.

The basic cake recipes in this book are based on an 8-inch cake pan, or 20 to 24 cupcakes, or 25 fondant fancies. Please bear in mind for each cake tier you will need 2 cakes, in other words, double the amount of cake batter, baked in 2 pans of the same size. The second column below indicates by how much the basic recipe needs to be divided or multiplied.

I also recommend baking a cake 1 inch larger than required, it will shrink during baking and the sides are usually a bit dry. After baking, trim the edges with a serrated knife down to the exact size required, using the cake board as a guide.

CAKE PAN SIZE (ROUND OR SQUARE)	QUANTITY OF BASIC RECIPE TO USE	CAKE PORTIONS 1x1 INCH ROUND/SQUARE	MINI CAKES	CUP-CAKES	FONDANT FANCIES
4 inches	¼	10 / 16			
5 inches	⅓	12 / 20			
6 inches	½	20 / 35			
7 inches	¾	25 / 45			
8 inches	1	40 / 60	9	20 to 24	25
9 inches	1⅓	50 / 80			
10 inches	2	60 / 100	16	40 to 48	36
11 inches	2½	80 / 120			
12 inches	3¼	90 / 140	25		
14 inches	4¼	130 / 185			

If you want a large centerpiece, but only need a small amount of cake, use a fake tier in between real tiers. Tell the bride and groom, to prevent them from trying to cut it.

QUANTITY GUIDE FOR MARZIPAN, ROLLED FONDANT ICING, AND BUTTERCREAM OR CHOCOLATE GANACHE FILLINGS

The figures below give you the approximate amounts required for cakes of different sizes, round or square, with a height of 3½ inches.

CAKE / BOARD SIZE	MARZIPAN/ ROLLED FON-DANT ICING	ROLLED FONDANT FOR CAKE BOARD	BUTTERCREAM/ GANACHE
4 inches	14 ounces		⅔ cup
			(also 25 fondant fancies)
5 inches	1 pound 2 ounces		1 cup
6 inches	1¼ pounds	10 ounces	1¼ cups
7 inches	1 pound 10 ounces	14 ounces	2 cups
			(also 20 to 24 cupcakes)
8 inches	1¾ pounds	1¼ pounds	2½ cups
			(also 25 mini cakes)
9 inches	2 pounds	23 ounces	3 cups
10 inches	2¾ pounds	27 ounces	4 cups
11 inches	3 pounds 3 ounces	1¾ pounds	5⅓ cups
12 inches	3½ pounds	2 pounds	3 pounds 3 ounces
13 inches	4½ pounds	2 pounds 2 ounces	3½ pounds
14 inches	5½ pounds	2¼ pounds	4½ pounds

Index

A
anemone cake 82–5
assembling tiered cakes 128–9

B
baking
   cakes 113–18
   cookies 110–12
ballerina pumps 8–9
baubles, Christmas 16–19
Belgian chocolate ganache 121
best in show cookies 12–13
blossom tints 109
boards, covering 127
bows
   dots and bows 54–5
   pretty bows 14–15
boxes, couture hatboxes 90–3
buttercream frosting 120
   layering cakes 124, 125–6
button flowers cake 96–9

C
cake boards, covering 127
cake pans, lining 113
cakes
   assembling tiered cakes 128–9
   baking 113–18
   carrot cake 117
   covering with marzipan 123–4, 126
   dipping 129–31
   icing 122–6
   large cakes 64–103
   layering cakes 122–6
   marble cake 118
   mini cakes 26–63
   rich dark chocolate cake 115–16
   Victoria sponge cake 114–15
cameo cakes 30–3
carrot cake 117
cherry blossom bites 42–5

chocolate
   Belgian chocolate ganache 121
   French fancies 60–3
   marble cake 118
   mochaccino dots 86–9
   rich dark chocolate cake 115–16
Christmas baubles cookies 16–19
Coco's corsage 94–5
colors 108–9

cookies 6–25
   baking 110–12
   ballerina pumps 8–9
   best-in-show 12–13
   Christmas baubles 16–19
   gingerbread cookies 111–12
   I want candy cookies 22–5
   little black dress 10–11
   pretty bows 14–15
   silhouette cookies 20–1
   sugar cookies 110–11
corsage, Coco's 94–5
couture hatboxes 90–3
covering cake boards 127
cream, Belgian chocolate ganache
  121
cupcakes
   cupcakes in bloom 50–3
   dipping 131

D
damask delights 28–9
dipping
   cup cakes 131
   fondant fancies 129–30
dogs
   best in show cookies 12–13
   pink poodle cake 76–81
dots
   dots and bows 54–5
   mochaccino dots 86–9
   piping 135
dowels, assembling tiered cakes 128–9
dress, little black 10–11
dusting colors 109

E
edible luster 109
equipment 106–7, 136

F
flowers
   anemone cake 82–5
   blossom tints 109
   button flowers cake 96–9
   cherry blossom bites 42–5
   Coco's corsage 94–5
   cupcakes in bloom 50–3
   mini orangery cakes 34–7
   pure white perfection 66–9

fondant fancies, dipping 129–30
food colors 108–9
French fancies 60–3
frosting, buttercream 120

G
ganache
   Belgian chocolate ganache 121
   layering cakes 124, 125–6
gingerbread cookies 111–12

H
handbags, Peggy's purses 46–9
hatboxes, couture 90–3
hydrangeas, cup cakes in bloom 50–3

I
I want candy cookies 22–5
ice crystal cakes 56–9
icing cakes 122–6
   buttercream frosting 120
   paper pastry bags 134
   piping techniques 135
   royal icing 132–3

L
large cakes 64–103
   anemone cake 82–5
   button flowers cake 96–9
   Coco's corsage 94–5
   couture hatboxes 90–3
   layering and icing 125–6
   mochaccino dots 86–9
   pink poodle 76–81
   pure white perfection 66–9
   summer symphony 70–5
   Tiffany pearl 100–3
layering cakes 122–6
leaves, mini orangery cakes 37
lemon syrup 119
letters, mini monogram cakes 39–41
lines, piping 135
lining cake pans 113
liquid fondant, dipping cakes 129–31
little black dress cookies 10–11
loops, piping 135
luster, edible 109

M
marble cake 118
marzipan, covering cakes with 123–4, 126

Acknowledgments

Developing the concept for *Cake Chic* has been an absolute joy and I am incredibly proud of the result. The idea was to create a range of fabulously stylish cake designs and recipes that us girls would love to make not only for special occasions, but also to make any occasion a little bit special. The result is a truly gorgeous collection of couture cookies and cakes, and I hope that you will feel inspired by them—perhaps even discover a new talent—and have lots of fun when baking and creating these recipes.

Of course, like all books, it was a joint effort. I would like to thank the great team at Quadrille Publishing—Jane O'Shea, Helen Lewis, and Katherine Case, headed by Alison Cathie! Thank you so much for all you support, input and creative guidance, and most important for sharing my vision for this wonderful new title. I hope you are all as delighted with the result as I am.

Another big thank-you goes to the rest of my hugely talented team, my lovely editor Lewis Esson, the incredible photographer Georgia Glynn Smith, and the stylish stylist Vicky Sullivan—for all the love, dedication, and inspiration you have brought to this project and for helping me to create this beautiful book.

To my new husband Bryn and my wonderful family—you give me the most incredible strength, love, and support that I couldn't do without, and I owe everything to you!

The publishers would also like to thank the following for their invaluable assistance: Liberty Art Fabrics, London www.liberty.co.uk <www.liberty.co.uk%20> for permission to reproduce the fabric featured on the endpapers and on pages 43 and 45; Cole & Son www.cole-and-son.com <http://www.cole-and-son.com> for the Catwalk wallpaper featured on page 77; Farrow & Ball www.Farrow-Ball.com <http://www.Farrow-Ball.com> for their Spencer wallpaper featured on page 82; Joanna Wood www.joannawood.co.uk <http://www.joannawood.co.uk> for the plates, coffee cup and saucer featured on page 10; www.NewVintage.co.uk <http://www.NewVintage.co.uk> for the vintage china featured on pages 15, 43 and 45, and 61 and 63; Rice www.rice.dk <http://www.rice.dk> for the plates featured on pages 74-5.

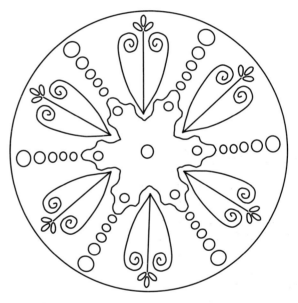

141

TEMPLATES FOR THE MINI MONOGRAM CAKES

DOWEL POSITIONS
FOR SQUARE CAKES

DOWEL POSITIONS
FOR ROUND CAKES

25cm (10")

20cm (8")

15cm (6")

10cm (4")

TEMPLATES FOR POSITIONING CAKE DOWELS, THE BALLET PUMPS
(TOP RIGHT) AND FOR THE PINK POODLE CAKE